TINKER'S MUFTI

TINKER'S MUFTI

Memoirs
of a part-time soldier
by
BASIL PEACOCK

Tinker's Mufti . . . A mixture of military
and civilian clothes worn together, which
is loathed by adjutants

LONDON
SEELEY SERVICE & CO

First published in Great Britain 1974 by
SEELEY SERVICE & COMPANY
196 Shaftesbury Avenue,
London W.C.2 H 8JL

COPYRIGHT © BASIL PEACOCK 1974

ISBN 0 85422 063 1

Printed in Great Britain by
Ebenezer Baylis & Son Ltd
The Trinity Press, Worcester, and London

Contents

Foreword 1

Chapter 1   INFANT NURTURE   *page*   3

BOY AT ARMS

Chapter 2   SCHOLAR IN A SOLDIER'S COAT   19
Chapter 3   THE FLEDGLING OFFICERS   43
Chapter 4   OFF TO THE WARS   47
Chapter 5   ALARMS AND EXCURSIONS   55
Chapter 6   CANNONADE AND CATASTROPHE   63
Chapter 7   IN AND OUT OF PRISON   76

THE LONG FURLOUGH

Chapter 8   STUDENT IN CIVVY STREET   91
Chapter 9   A MUSTERING OF SOLDIERS   104

MIDDLE AGE AT WAR

Chapter 10 'AUX ARMES, CITOYENS!'   121
Chapter 11 TROOPING TO THE TROPICS   133
Chapter 12 DOUBTS, DEFEAT AND DISASTER   155
Chapter 13 CAPTIVE ON THE KWAI   171

ENGLAND, HOME AND ABROAD AGAIN

Chapter 14   ENGLAND, HOME AND ABROAD AGAIN   *185*

ROADS BACK

Chapter 15   SLOW BOAT TO THE ORIENT   *193*
Chapter 16   LES COMBATANTS ANCIENS   *199*
Chapter 17   FAREWELL TO ARMS   *210*

Appendix 213

Illustrations

between pages 38 and 39

1. The author, 1912
2. Uncle Archie
3. The Peacock Family in 1899
4. Soldiers Three, 1915
5. The Cooks, Royal Fusiliers, Edinburgh, 1916
6. The author, private, Royal Fusiliers, 1916
7. The author, 2nd Lieutenant, Northumberland Fusiliers, 1917
8. The author as a Major in the TA, 1939
9. The author on his return from the Far East, 1945
10. Officers of the 32nd Coy, 31st S/L Bn, RE, 1934
11. 14th S/L Battery RA, Changi, 1941

between pages 166 and 167

12. On the Kwai Railway, 1944
13. The author reunited with his son
14. HRH The Duchess of Kent, Borneo, 1952
15. Twenty years after—the author and his wife revisit Thailand
16. Ex-soldiers three; Jim, the author and Alex

Foreword

Books and autobiographies by great personages and eminent people who have left their mark on history are abundant, but this is the story of the life of an ordinary man during the closing years of the nineteenth and seventy years of the twentieth century.

It is said that 'every man has a book in him and one day in his life makes a page of his history'. The pages of this, my book, may have recorded only prosaic and minor happenings, but together with many thousands of my generation I was caught up in the great wars and events of the first half of the twentieth century; and these five decades are probably the most interesting, critical and progressive in known history.

Those of my generation, born in the reign of Queen Victoria, have seen more social changes than at any other time in English history; and other changes — in transport, from pony and trap to supersonic flight; from mechanical panoramas and magic lanterns to colour television; from simple telegraph to signals from satellites and the moon. There have even been changes in the definitions of right and wrong, and what were termed virtues and simple faiths. A supposedly puritanical society has become a supposedly permissive one.

So many lives were affected by the great historical happenings of this era that many readers of this book will, at times, identify themselves with my experiences. By chance and a little waywardness, these experiences have been diverse and varied, so that few readers will have lived as I have; but I know that someone, somewhere, perusing a paragraph in my text, will look up from the book and exclaim, 'That is just what happened to me and these were my thoughts.'

Many younger readers may feel that my generation lived in a barbaric, unjust and unhappy society, which willingly engaged in two bloodbaths and killed off the most promising youth of the time. A few shallow-thinking, noisy protesters may feel that wars, even defensive ones, are crimes against humanity, and that 'imperialism' was a cruel and wicked system, not realizing that British success in both war and Empire-building ensured their freedom to protest and contributed to the present affluence, luxury, and security in their lives.

However, I know from association with them that many charming, intelligent young people are intensely interested in the activities of my generation, and that the study of our times is becoming popular, even 'trendy'. We ancients may be referred to as 'squares', laughed at a little sometimes, pitied; but—I wonder—are these young men and women just a little jealous of our experiences and memories?

Few of my contemporaries are jealous of the mode of life of the young, in many ways more complicated and jading than ours. True, sixty-odd years ago, life was hard for most people, if they were not of the aristocracy or moneyed classes; but we had our diversions, and our pleasures were mostly home-made, not coming in pre-packaged lots or over the ether, and we enjoyed them as much as modern amusements.

So there is not the slightest need for pity or concern, as nearly one hundred per cent of my generation declare that they are grateful to belong to it, to have taken part in great historical events, and are not in the least bit envious of those destined to live their lives in this atomic age, this polluted, technological 'Brave new world'.

Chapter 1

INFANT NURTURE

My advent into a large, impecunious, strict Presbyterian family was something of a surprise, as most relatives were under the impression that the family had been completed some years before.

I was born at home — 19 Cheltenham Terrace, Newcastle-upon-Tyne — on 2nd April, 1898, a Saturday's child, under the sign of Aries, the Ram. Everyone knew the old rhyme 'Saturday's child must work hard for his living', but few people in those days knew anything about signs of the Zodiac; newspapers did not feature them or give horoscopes. Yet the sign turned out to be curiously appropriate, as astrologers pronounce that babies born under Aries are destined for struggle, hardship, soldiering and war. I was a most unlikely infant for a future which was to include much soldiering, as I was a most tearful child and a little timid, for no apparent reason as for years I led a sheltered life as the baby of our large family.

My parents, who had produced six offspring before my arrival (the first died in infancy), were running out of names, having given each child two, and later in life I was told that I was christened 'Basil' — only one forename — after a boy whose adventures were being described in *The Captain* magazine at the time of my birth. It has been a sad handicap for most of my life, being an unusual name in our stratum of society, and looked upon in the rough, industrial Tyneside town as effeminate or 'cissy', and I suffered accordingly. Quite recently, I learned that it means 'kingly', which would have embarrassed me even more at school, as I was always small for my age and not in the least regal.

My mother, née Jane Briggs, a small, tough lady of old Tyneside stock, came from a family of deep-sea sailors and river keelmen, and one of the first songs I learned was, 'Weel may the keel row that my laddie's in'. Early photographs show her as a comely woman, with a trim figure in a tight-buttoned bodice and a looped skirt with a small bustle. She was a wonderful manager, though a little slapdash at times. She rarely had time to sit down and rest, having so much to do looking after us and cleaning our six-roomed house. This was furnished in true Victorian style, with draperies on the mantelpieces, covers on the tables, and sort of frilled pantaloons on the chair legs. There were horse-hair sofas, grandfather's easy chairs with antimacassars, and tinkling glass lustres on shelves, all of which required much attention and dusting.

On washing days, a woman helper arrived wearing a man's flat cap secured by a hat-pin, which seemed to be de rigueur for those in this class of work, the house would be filled with steam from an enormous copper in which the clothes were boiled. They were then given rude treatment with a poss-stick in a large tub: a poss-stick was a stout pole with a cross-piece handle with at the business end an enormous hollowed-out, cylindrical piece of heavy wood. Meals on washing days were a bit sketchy and always tasted of steam and Lifebuoy soap.

Mother received very little housekeeping money, but she brought up her family well fed, decently clothed and what she called 'respectable'. She also brought us up as staunch teetotallers, as she was a keen member of The British Women's Temperance Association. Nearly all the family eventually became lapsed teetotallers, even after long membership in the Sons of Temperance — a strictly non-alcoholic society for children. Nevertheless, Mother constantly brewed large quantities of supposedly non-alcoholic ginger beer and dandelion stout in her pantry. The stone jars in which this was kept often blew their corks and occasionally exploded due to intense fermentation; I now know that the alcoholic

4

content of the brews must have exceeded that of any liquor on sale. Mother would have been horrified if she had realized this, as she pressed it on all visitors and enjoyed it herself.

She could be a tartar if vexed, and her favourite oath was 'By the living Harry' (referring either to Henry the Eighth or Harry Hotspur of Alnwick, but I doubt if she was aware of this). At times of great financial stress, which was frequent, she would remark bravely, 'Well, as one door shuts, another opens,' a maxim that has often cheered me in desperate times.

My father, James, a lean kindly sensitive man, mainly self-educated after attendance at a Dame School — fees two-pence a week — and a year or two at a Mission School in The Friar's Hall, was a great reader of the classics. He spent nothing on himself and could afford only one pastime, which was running, at which he excelled and won many prizes. Very occasionally, he rode a penny farthing bicycle. He kept a small provision shop which was always on the edge of bankruptcy, for he was a man of such honesty and integrity that he could not compete with smarter tradesmen and the growing competition of the Co-operative Stores.

My father should never have been in business for himself, although he was always proud to proclaim himself his own master. Given the opportunity, he would have made a great scholar and possibly a university professor, as indeed one son and two grandsons later became.

Few persons outside the schools and 'varsities' knew more of the works of the English poets than he did, and he made a special study of Shakespeare. I owe my love of books and memory for verse to him. At times he seemed a timorous man, but he was not afraid to stand up for justice or to express an unpopular opinion if he was convinced in his own mind. When our minister delivered his first sermon after his appointment, my father told him, 'Sir, I have to confess that I gained no spiritual uplift from your discourse.'

He selected his words like Dr Johnson did, and he could be a menace at political meetings; these he took very seriously, attending both Liberal and Tory gatherings with an open mind. His favourite question, delivered very courteously and mildly, was, 'Sir, having heard your views on matters of policy, can you please inform me why you feel yourself to have the necessary qualities to legislate for me and other members of the audience?'

He rarely obtained a satisfactory answer.

These two parents, denying themselves almost every luxury and some necessities, managed, with a little help from the state, to put four of their children through university, and there is little doubt that they counted the success of their offspring as ample reward for their early struggles. They themselves never did attain affluence, but they had some comfort late in life. Like most of their generation, they valued their independence and were self-reliant. They were in their late seventies before they were persuaded to accept the 'Old Age Pension' or 'Lloyd George's Dole', to which they had been entitled years before.

Despite our penury and enforced thrift, the family was looked upon in the neighbourhood as reasonably prosperous, mainly because we were decently dressed; in those days in an industrial town, always smoke-begrimed, the bulk of the population were ill-clad and often unwashed, anyway on weekdays. The working men were factory hands, pitmen, shipyard workers and artisans. White-collar workers were comparatively few, and tradesmen, office workers and particularly council employees were counted as well-to-do. Their children always had boots to wear, while many working-class children went barefoot, even in winter. Many homes were miserable places, and the working men spent their little spare time and cash in public houses or playing pitch-and-toss, a gambling game using halfpennies. They worked long and hard, and when they played did it wholeheartedly. On Saturdays, the gutters were strewn with helpless drunks; but the police were usually tolerant, delivering the culprits to their homes rather than charging them. The pitmen, delving and sweating miles underground, were a race apart; they took their beer in quarts, needing the liquid to replace the copious perspiration they lost during working hours. Though ill-paid and sometimes ill-used, they were proud of their hazardous occupation, accepting it as a challenge to their manhood. Their womenfolk understood this, too, and were proud of them.*

The people of north-east England in the ancient Kingdom of Northumbria have little Saxon or Norman blood in them; their forebears come mostly from Scandinavia and Friesland. Indeed, their peculiar dialect, almost incomprehensible to southerners, is related to Norwegian. They were and are clannish and fond of their birthplace, many returning there after long exile in more salubrious places and climates, proud of their undoubted skill as artisans and engineers. Throughout the history of the North, they have been known for speaking their minds to those in high places, often imprudently, but without fear. William the Conqueror was forced to ravage the country before he subdued them; and he then built numerous strongholds to help them in keeping out the Scots raiders. Under a cover of rough words, they are deeply sentimental, and because of this, they are happy to fight for a lost cause or to champion an unworthy underdog.

Nevertheless, for all their faults and what appear to be rough manners, these are 'canny folk'. On Tyneside the word 'canny' means basically kind and good-hearted — not 'thrifty', as it does in Scotland; and for a baby to be referred to as a 'canny little bairn' is very complimentary. For a man to be referred to as a 'canny bugger' is praise indeed, for this latter dubious noun is very commonplace in the North-east and is used as a term of endearment.

This, then, was the society into which I was born and in which I spent my boyhood. The older I grow, the more I remember about it, for we have long memories in the North. It is said that 'if you scratch a Northumbrian, you will find an antiquary'. Old customs and old expressions die hard there; and so do the people who, because of little pampering in early life and because of the climate, acquire physiques resilient to hardship, even at advanced ages. It is possibly

* 'The collier lad is a canny lad
He's always of good cheer
He knows how to work and knows how to shirk
And he knows how to sup his beer.'

due to these factors that I, too, have survived some hard conditions during my lifetime without much hurt.

People in our stratum of society had little spare money, so most of our entertainments were home-made and simple. A high spot in our lives was the annual Sunday school excursion for children, when we were taken a few miles into the country in horse charabancs to have a picnic and organized races.

In addition to Christmas, there were two feast days — Carling Sunday and Easter Day, and we used to count the Sundays before them by this rhyme:

'Tid, Mid, Misere
Carling, Palm,
and Paste Egg Day.'

The name 'Carling Sunday' has a curious origin. Carlings are a kind of grey pea which were eaten in great quantities, usually from paper bags, to commemorate the great siege of Newcastle during the great rebellion, when a ship, laden with these peas, broke the blockade and brought food to the starving townsfolk. Easter Day was called 'Paste Egg Day' — a corruption of *'pâques'*; mothers hardboiled dozens of eggs, colouring the shells with various dyes, onion-skins or cochineal, and presented them to friends, receiving one in return. Children might receive as many as a dozen each, and it was customary to hold 'jowping' competitions (striking the pointed ends one against another) to discover the toughest. During the afternoon, the children were dispatched to parks and open places to roll their eggs, a simple game to discover how far an egg would roll down a hill before breaking, and ending with the consumption of as many as little stomachs could tolerate.

There was another interesting custom which included the presentation of eggs. When a baby was being carried to church for his christening, usually in the grandmother's arms, the first stranger of the opposite sex to the infant met on the way was stopped and presented with an egg, a piece of wood, and a piece of silver wrapped in tissue paper! The stranger had to accept these, however surprised or reluctant; they were forced on this person even if he or she was not acquainted with the custom, for non-acceptance would bring bad luck to the baby. As recently as 1947, one of my sisters received such gifts from an old lady carrying a baby, in the suburbs of Newcastle.

The first entertainment I recall, for which one had to pay, was a panorama display in the town hall. It was mainly educational and consisted of a series of enormous canvases depicting scenes from Switzerland and Italy passing across a stage from one roller to another. The scenes were brilliantly coloured and lit, and a man gave a running commentary as they passed across. Towards the end of the performance, he announced that for the first time in Newcastle actual moving pictures would be shown on a screen. I remember that the actors in them looked foreign and appeared to be moving in heavy rainstorms. A few years later, moving pictures were shown in our church hall for the benefit of children in the Band of Hope. I remember seeing the first epic film, *The Great Train Robbery*, and being terrified when the steam engine seemed to be coming off the screen and into the audience.

Our church, Heaton Presbyterian, which still maintains a fair congregation, was the focal point of entertainment as well as being a place for worship and for gossip. After evening service, groups would visit each other's houses and sing lusty hymns around a piano. In our house the hymns were rousing revivalist types, as my mother was what was called at the time a 'Ranter' and declared, as did the Salvation Army, 'Why should the devil have all the best tunes?' I sometimes wonder if my proclivity for soldiering was induced by those early days, as nearly all were marching tunes with martial words, most of which I still recall. One of my favourites was 'Hold the Fort for I am Coming', and as an infant I used to think that this had something to do with the defence of Rorke's Drift, which was fresh in the minds of my elders and often discussed. In other sacred songs, there were exhortations to 'gird your armour on'; 'to lift high the royal banner, it must not suffer loss'; and we were always 'marching off to war'. Several of these hymns, with different words, became First World War soldiering songs: I wonder how many people now realize that 'Old soldiers never die' was cribbed from the hymn 'Kind words will never die', and 'Swinging the lead, boys, swinging the lead, the corporals are watching you swinging the lead' from 'Looking this way, yes, looking this way, the angels are watching you looking this way'.

With little thought of ever becoming one, I nevertheless developed an interest in soldiers at a very early age; one of my earliest recollections has to do with them. I was barely three years old at the time, and I remember waking up one night because of a commotion in the street below. Looking out of the bedroom window, I saw my mother on the pavement waving a Union Jack, which seemed an extraordinary thing for her to be doing. Next morning, I learned that some volunteer soldiers, who had been fighting some people called Boers, had returned and had been given a reception. This was very exciting, and I became even more excited when I discovered some pictures in a magazine of soldiers in pointed helmets with diagrammatic shells bursting around them.

My next contact with the military came a few years later when my Uncle Archie arrived back from Cape Colony, where he had served as a lieutenant in some very irregular cavalry. In 1879 he had enlisted as a trooper in the 17th Lancers—the Death or Glory Boys, and we had a picture of him in our family photograph album, resplendent in dress uniform, taken in Lucknow in the early eighties. I remember being very disappointed to see him dressed only in a blue serge suit.

Uncle Archie influenced me and my brothers in many ways since he was an interesting man and a good raconteur, quite unlike other members of the family. He was a fine amateur artist and musician but was too indolent to make money from these gifts. By nature he took things calmly, and his service in the tropics led him to idleness and procrastination. On being pressed by his wife to get on with some urgent job, he would remark 'Tuts, woman, why now? There's all next week not used up yet.'

During his visits to our house, I would avoid being sent to bed by keeping quiet behind a sofa so that I could listen to his stories. He had joined the ranks, rather precipitously, after some peccadillo, as so many recruits did in those days, and always pretended to have been a reluctant soldier. He often told us that when he was lying on his cot on his first night as a recruit at Canterbury Depot, he stared up at the lances standing upright against the walls and said to himself, 'I'll desert in the morning.' He would then pause till some- one asked, 'Why didn't you, Uncle?', and reply, 'I never got the confounded time, what with cleaning myself, uniform and harness and grooming horses, I never got a minute to myself for twelve long years. Never join the cavalry, boys — those blasted long-faced animals simply eat men, as well as forage.'

He was on parade at a public hanging of a British soldier in India — perhaps that described by Kipling in his verses 'Danny Deever' — and told the tale as follows:

'When I was in the 17th Lancers in India, a private of a line regiment was court-martialled for shooting his sergeant dead — I think it was something to do with a woman. He was sentenced to be hanged in front of the whole garrison for the good of discipline, and one steaming hot morning, we were paraded in full dress on the barrack square where a platform and gallows had been built and covered with black cloth in the middle. The drums of the bands were draped in black and all the troops wore black armbands. We lancers were on foot carrying our lances. When the condemned man was brought out on to the square with his escort and the padre, the drums tapped a slow march and then the Provost-Marshal read out the sentence. The prisoner did not seem to care what was happening, but the troops were dropping down fainting in dozens and we were all sweating in rivers. I would have fallen down myself if I had not leaned heavily on my lance. The hangman did his horrible job quickly and immediately we were marched off with the bands playing something like the Dead March and returned to our quarters.'

Oddly enough, this was not the end of the story, for thirty years afterwards my uncle was in a pub in Newcastle when he heard an old man telling some young fellows about the execution. They did not believe the tale, called him a liar and began teasing him. Uncle spoke to the old chap, saying that he believed him as he was present on parade, serving in the 17th Lancers.

'That's right,' said the old man, 'there was only some sappers and commissaries, our ould regiment and some cavalry in the cantonment. Now to prove ye was there, and I was not lying, tell these youngsters what was the last thing the condemned man did before going up the steps to the gallows.'

My uncle replied, 'I shall never forget it — he shook hands with the sentry at the foot of the steps.'

The old man looked round at his listeners and exclaimed, 'Sor, I was in the infantry at that time — and I was that sentry.'

During my uncle's service in India, Kipling began to write his *Barrack Room Ballads* and *Soldiers Three* stories in the *Lahore Gazette*, and Uncle Archie read them avidly. In some ways he could have been a character in them; older people in our part of the country found him very different from themselves and referred to him as 'a proper caution'.

Mother was always a little distant towards Uncle Archie and tried to lessen our interest in him. She considered him the black sheep of our clan, as ranker soldiers in those days were looked upon as being only one step removed from convicts. This was a common opinion then, and it is true that most of the men were pretty tough customers, given to lewd language and tippling. There was a small garrison at Fenham Barracks, Newcastle, and one often saw soldiers — 'swaddies' was the popular name for them — walking about town in colourful uniforms, with fore-and-aft caps and swagger canes. They all wore pointed waxed moustaches and were straight-backed and upright, except when in drink. They looked like my idea of soldiers, but in times of peace they were derided and looked upon as vulgar loafers. Many public houses would not serve them with drink, and they were driven to the less respectable taverns in slummier parts of the town. However, only a few years later these same derided men formed part of the 'Contemptible Little

Army' which fought and died with such courage at Mons and on the Marne.

Once a year the troops gave a small military display on the town moor, curiously enough at a Temperance Festival, and as my father was on the committee, our family got good seats to view it. I used to stare fascinated at the precision drill, the tent-pegging and musical rides, never dreaming that within a few years I would be wearing a uniform and learning my drill.

When I was eight years old, I met a soldier even older than my uncle; I was walking in the public park with my father when he stopped to speak to an old acquaintance, a tall upright man with a limp who carried a stout stick. My father said, 'Shake hands with this gentleman, Basil. I want you to remember this meeting always. Mr —— is an old soldier, a Crimean War veteran who was nursed by the Lady of the Lamp, Miss Florence Nightingale, whom you have read about in your school books.'

As I have been involved with soldiers for most of my life, it is odd that I never played at soldiers with my friends, though I used to sit on my rocking horse and wave a tin sword about, much to my mother's annoyance. In fact, I was not one for outdoor games, until I went to high school, but spent long hours indoors reading. Before I was ten, I had read most of the books of Mark Twain, delighting in *Huckleberry Finn* and *Tom Sawyer*, also some of Dickens and had even attempted Scott. I read 'Tales of the Outposts' in *Blackwood's Magazine* when other children were reading fairy stories, never dreaming that I should write tales like them later in life. My brothers bought the *Boys' Own Paper* in weekly numbers, and I read some good stuff in those, including 'The Fifth Form at St Dominics', by Talbot Baines Read, and adventure stories by Henty. When I could obtain it, I preferred the paper *Chums* in which the stories were much more bloodsome and generally about soldiers or pirates, but in our home this paper was considered undesirable for boys.

I was called a bookworm long before I understood what the term meant. I think it was my elder brother, irritated

13

by my reluctance to go out to play, who remarked, 'If you like adventures, you must go out and seek them; that's what the word means. Don't wait for adventures to come to you.' How right he was.

The exciting things that did happen may seem trivial to my grandsons but to me then they were almost in the class of adventures. One day near our church I saw my first motor-car and ran after it till I was exhausted; I was taken to London to see the Franco-Britain Exhibition and was given a special treat, a ride down the Strand on a motor-bus instead of on the usual horse-driven vehicle. A doctor's son, an advanced young man, gave me a ride in a sort of wickerwork basket, a side-car to his motor-bike, terrifying my mother. Some years later, I glimpsed a Bleriot-type aeroplane flying over the town moor, coming in to land at Gosforth Park Racecourse.

When I was about ten years old, our family rented a farm — a labourer's cottage in a tiny hamlet in an isolated part of Northumberland — for four pounds a year; we children were dispatched there at holiday times to live a cheap, bucolic existence. We generally walked the ten miles from the railway station as there was no other means of trans-port, except the postman's trap, but he charged one shilling and sixpence per trip which was much too expensive. No one thought it unusual for a small boy to make this journey on foot, and the exercise probably increased my stamina. The cottage was adjacent to fell country, and my brothers occasionally acted as beaters in the grouse season. I played with farm lads beside a lovely gurgling river a few hundred yards from the house, where we tried to catch fish and got soaked to the skin sailing on rough rafts of logs. We helped in the fields, getting in the hay, and rode delightedly on the hay bogies — low sideless carts which replaced hay wains in that part of the country. Since that time I may have spent hundreds of pounds on one short holiday, but I have rarely enjoyed it as much as these which cost only a few shillings. That tiny village is unchanged to this day, and to help keep it that way I do not want to give its name or location.

It was in 1912, during one of these holidays in the country, that I first heard the rumblings of coming war. The postman had delivered a newspaper, and my brother Jim, ten years older than I, looked up from reading it and announced that England would have to go to war with Germany over something called the Agadir crisis. I was alarmed when he said he would have to go and fight; I could not understand what it was all about, or even what a crisis meant. Jim seemed to be a most unlikely man to be a soldier, as he is a gentle, kind person with no war-like proclivities. Later, I learned that he had already joined the university OTC at Newcastle, where he was an undergraduate, after hearing a lecture by Mr Haldane, the War Minister who was responsible for creating the Territorial Army. My eldest brother, Alex, had already joined the volunteers — 'K' Company of the 6th Battalion, the Northumberland Fusiliers, which was comprised of university students. But since Mother hated to see them in their uniforms, they rarely put them on in the house.

I soon forgot about the Agadir crisis, having gained a part-scholarship to Rutherford College, a sort of grammar school, mainly because of a story I wrote in an examination. At first I did quite well at this establishment, until I was given accelerated promotion and placed in what is now termed the 'science stream'; here I almost drowned, as no one could be less of a scientist than me. The school concentrated on producing engineers, physicists, marine architects, chemists and teachers for the industries, and the Humanities came a poor second. Only one master, Mr Tommy Moles, who taught the Humanities and the Classics in some isolation, seemed to detect my inclination thereto, but by then it was too late.

I was struggling to keep my place at the bottom of the sixth form, to which I had been unwisely promoted, when the First World War came upon us, and life was never the same again.

BOY AT ARMS

Chapter 2

SCHOLAR IN A SOLDIER'S COAT

FEW of my school-fellows at this time knew anything about the actual causes of the war or about the events leading up to hostilities. We had heard about the assassination of an Austrian archduke, but that was about all. Boys rarely read newspapers in those days, nor did every household regularly take a paper, although they might buy the occasional copy from a newsboy in the street. We could not miss the placards with headlines about Germans and the Kaiser, and we did see the cartoons; but none of us could have given a good reason why our country should declare war. We simply found it very exciting.

I remember experiencing a great thrill as I watched two men pasting up an announcement on our church notice-board. It was coloured red, white and blue and was headed 'General Mobilization'; it announced that all Army Reservists and Territorials must report to their head-quarters immediately, and ended with the words 'God Save the King'.

Few of us had any knowledge of Germans, except those who played in German bands; these were a common sight in the streets before 1914. They wore a grey uniform and pork-pie hats with tiny peaks, not unlike those of German infantry NCOs. These bands were rather popular, as they played jolly tunes, so the collections they took up were fairly generous. In the North country also, there were many pork shops under the management of Germans, and these too were popular, as they supplied delicious hot and cold meats and pease pudding—favourite foods for the working class since they were both appetizing and cheap. Boys such as myself would buy 'a ha'penny dip' consisting of two halves of a substantial bread bun dipped in hot pork fat with a morsel of crackling between them, which reduced the pangs of hunger between meals. Suddenly these kindly pork butchers were turned into ogres and suspected spies, as their compatriots marched across Europe, sacking its cities and committing terrible atrocities. It was in Newcastle that I saw my first act of war, when a famous pork shop owned by Germans who had lived in the town for two generations was looted by a mob from the slums—mostly women, and the family was taken away into protective custody.

To the pupils of Rutherford College, the first impact of the war was the sudden departure of our French master, M. Maubouson, to join his Regiment of Chasseurs, of which he became adjutant. He sent us a photograph of himself wearing a kepi, a long blue overcoat, red trousers and a sword. A few weeks later, at Assembly, we were shocked to hear our headmaster announce that he had been killed in action—the first of many casualties from our school.

One or two of the older boys from the Upper Sixth left school, since they were members of the RNVR or the Territorial Army. My elder brother, Alex, then a lecturer at Durham University, joined the 50th Field Ambulance. He tried first to enlist in the infantry, but he was turned down because of poor eyesight. Soon after, my other brother, Jim, newly married, enlisted in the University and Public Schools Brigade of the Royal Fusiliers. This brigade was raised to attract a certain type of recruit, and in many ways it was a mistake on the part of the military authorities, as most of the personnel were officer material and were badly needed elsewhere a few months later. It served as an ordinary infantry formation and lost many men who should have been leading others in the new Kitchener's Army. Both my brothers had been in the OTC and should have waited for commissions, but at that time it was still thought that an officer needed a private income to supplement his pay.

The recruiting posters, especially the well-known one showing Kitchener pointing at the reader, with the caption 'Your Country Needs YOU', were most effective. Soon tens of thousands of men of military age, and many who falsified their ages, besieged the recruiting offices to enlist.

Protesting youth of today may ask 'Why did they do so, knowing so little of the *casus belli*?' The answer is simple. They were patriotic, thinking it their duty to fight for King and Country; moreover, they felt they would be unable to face their relatives and friends after the war if they had taken no part in it. Another reason, of course, was that it was an exciting contrast to their humdrum lives. As Dr Johnson succinctly put it two centuries ago:

'Every man thinks meanly of himself for not having been a soldier or not having been at sea.'

Truly 'all the youth of England was on fire', but none of them foresaw that the fire of their enthusiasm would be reduced to a few glowing embers before hostilities ceased. Few thought that the war would last four years, although Kitchener thundered that it would take three years to defeat the German might; most people thought it would be all over by Christmas.

C. E. Montague, in his book *Disenchantment*, wrote about the spirit of the response to the call to arms: 'there was something divine about it'; and certainly no youth or adult who lived through that time can forget the atmosphere. Although there was a section of the population, some of the intelligentsia, who detested the idea of war for any reason, I can remember at the school only one boy, who came from a family of Fabians, who said that war was foolish and wicked, and that he would never take part in it. Oddly enough, we excused his attitude on the grounds that he was physically unfit, thinking his remarks were sour grapes.

At that time I was just sixteen, the youngest and smallest in the Sixth Form. One or two older boys who had already passed the matriculation exam and were waiting to go to the university, joined the university OTC, and in a surprisingly short time blossomed into second lieutenants. They were looked upon with envy by the remainder of the form when they visited the school in their uniforms. Poor boys, they were of that generation which was almost completely wiped out before they attained their twenty-first birthdays. I have a photograph of our rugby football team for 1914, in which I am included as scrum-half. To my knowledge, only four of the players in this team survived the war. Three friends with whom I regularly walked to school during 1914 were killed before they were twenty.

I think it was the sight of school-fellows in uniform which made me determined to wear one too. I cannot say that I have ever been particularly belligerent; and, curiously, throughout my service, I never realized that I personally might have to kill anybody. I have thought a great deal about this in later life, and can only believe that it was the pageantry and panoply of military life in war and peace that attracted me to soldiering. Even now, at the age of seventy-four, the sound of a military band and the sight of marching soldiers stirs me deeply.

I began my military career in 1915 by joining a curious organization called the Junior Training League, which was founded by several town councillors and retired soldiers who were too old themselves to fight. They realized that there were scores of boys like myself, too young to enlist but keen to train as soldiers; and so they advertised in the local papers, directing that any such should report to the town hall assembly room on a certain evening. The response was astounding, almost comic, and the elderly founders were engulfed in a seething mob of boys clamouring to join. When I arrived, there were hundreds inside and hundreds more fighting to get in. It was like a modern students' demo, and the councillors had to take refuge on a high platform. The noise in the hall was terrific until an old gentleman in the uniform of a reserve colonel came on to the stage and with lungs of brass shouted, 'Boys, if you want to be soldiers, the first thing you must learn is who is boss. I am going to be your boss and commanding officer, and I intend to teach you obedience immediately.'

22

The pandemonium stilled, and he continued, 'All we can do tonight is to take the names of keen lads. These will form an orderly queue and give their names and addresses to my NCOs. They will throw out any skylarkers or disorderly boys immediately. There will be further orders in the newspapers. Quietly, now.'

We remained quiet. I managed to get my name down and left the hall with another boy, who became my friend and companion in arms for many years. His name was Roland Wood, and he was the eldest of a military family whose charm and amusing eccentricities have continued to enchant me over the years.

My parents were unenthusiastic about the Junior Training League but relieved to find that I had taken on no military obligations; they probably thought that this occupation would take the fidgets out of me. They reminded me that I was supposed to be studying for my matriculation and that I should not neglect my books by spending too much time learning drill.

The Training League soon got underway, and we were given a piece of red, white and blue cord to wear in the shoulder-seam of our jackets to indicate membership. It was the first quasi-military badge that I acquired, and it gave me more pride than real ones did later. Within a few weeks, about fifty of us were given a written examination on simple military subjects for the purpose of selecting NCOs. I came top in this, the only time I did so in any examination, and Roland came second. Our success was due to the fact that we had a little education and were literate; many of the boys could read or write only with difficulty. Roland was made Cadet Company Sergeant Major, and I was made a Platoon Sergeant. Our troops were keen enough; some slacked, but when a few miniature rifles were produced, we fought for the honour of carrying them to the range. I fired my first live ammunition at the Elswick factory miniature range in 1915, and I still fire a few shots at Bisley each year.

During the summer of 1915, I presented myself for the matriculation examination of Durham University and to my astonishment obtained a pass. Though marvelling at my success, I was a little peeved that so many others marvelled at it also. Our chemistry master, a good teacher, but much given to sarcasm, called me out in front of the form and said in a loud voice, 'There is a rumour about the school that you, Peacock, have actually passed your matriculation examination. Pray let me hear the truth from your own lips.'

Reddening, I stammered 'It is true, sir.'

He paused a moment and said, 'Great heavens! Then this is one of the most remarkable results I have ever heard. Go back; resume your seat.'

He gave me not one word of praise or congratulation, and — may this be a warning to sarcastic teachers — I still feel sour about it fifty-seven years later.

Having matriculated, I was now eligible to join the university OTC; but my application was turned down, and I was told to grow a bit. However, a few months later, with the help of a colleague of my brother's, I was accepted. I was sent to report to a squad drilling on the town moor under a massive sergeant-major. He looked at me, examined the chit I had delivered to him and summoned a sergeant to whom he exclaimed, 'Look what they are sending us now as cadets, bloody babies!'

He checked my chit again, then shouted, 'Right, join that bloody squad and get some ginger in your backside, and grow, boy!'

He was slightly mollified when he saw that my arms drill, which I had learned in the Junior Training League, was of a fair standard.

Cadets had to pay a small subscription to belong to the corps, even in wartime, and also to buy their own uniforms, khaki tunic with black buttons, breeches and puttees. Our cap badge, in black, was the St Cuthbert's Cross. We also had to pay our expenses at week-end camps, which consisted mainly of digging trenches in foul weather; and it was thus that I spent three of the wettest and muddiest days of my life, in the wilds of Northumberland, having paid fifteen shillings for the privilege. I arrived home dead beat and soaked to the skin; my mother was thoroughly alarmed and could not believe that I had enjoyed myself.

By this time, I had been persuaded by my parents to follow my brother's profession and become a teacher — 'a nice, steady and respectable occupation' — and as I had nothing else to do, I eventually got myself an appointment as a pupil teacher at an elementary school. I hated it from the first day. I was told nothing about how to teach. I was simply placed in charge of a mixed class of boys and girls, not much younger than myself, some of whom looked rather older. My own knowledge of several subjects in the curriculum was no better than theirs. One lad soon spotted this and deliberately asked me devilishly awkward questions to which he knew the answer and I did not. He was a boy with a high IQ, and he eventually became a top civil servant with a knighthood; perhaps I can take some credit for this success since he used me to sharpen his wits!

Many years later, after I married, I was dancing with a young lady when she remarked, to my horror, 'You know, you used to teach me. You were a scream, you couldn't teach for nuts, could you?'

Seeing my dismay, she continued, 'But all the girls liked you in your uniform, and some of us were a little in love with you.'

I agreed with her first remark and was cheered by her second; I explained that at the time I didn't have a decent suit to wear, having just grown out of boys' clothes, and had no alternative but to wear the uniform.

I determined to get out of teaching at any price, and as soon as I was seventeen and a half I applied for a commission. At that time one could be accepted for a Special Reserve appointment; but just before time came for me to appear in front of the selection board, the regulations were changed so that no one under nineteen years of age could be appointed an officer. My friend Roland Wood had been commissioned at the age of eighteen since his father, a lieutenant on the Reserve, had introduced him to an old commanding officer of his. I did appear before the selection board; they saw that I was very disappointed, and one officer said kindly,

'There are other ways of getting into the army. We want recruits, and in time you may become an officer.'

I was so chagrined by my failure to qualify that I decided that I would indeed join the ranks if possible, without my parents' knowledge. Since the recruiting posters told one to call personally, I went to the barracks. Here a recruiting sergeant, learning my age, rubbed his chin thoughtfully and said, 'You could perhaps join as a boy in the regulars, for about fifteen years, if you have your parents' consent. Pity you are not nineteen. Why not think about it?'

I went back the next day, saw the same recruiting sergeant, and said I was nineteen. I then went before the Medical Officer who also asked my age. I replied, 'Nineteen today, sir.'

'Is that so?' he replied. He gave me a hasty examination with a stethoscope, directed me to read a sight card, and then continued, 'I don't believe you, but you are fit enough.' He then signed my papers.

I went home, and telling a few fibs, I said I had been accepted as a boy-soldier. There was not as serious a row as I had expected; my mother, looking sad, simply said, 'Isn't it enough that your two brothers have gone?'

My father looked as though he did not believe me and remarked severely, 'You have been moody and difficult for a long time. Now you have made your own bed, you must lie on it.'

I thought of one thing in my defence, something which had prompted me to enlist immediately. I told them that many others had done as I had done, and that if I waited much longer I should anyway be conscripted (conscription was now certain). I wanted to be a volunteer like my brothers. This argument paid off. A few days later, in my father's shop, I heard a customer bemoaning the fact that her sons would be called up. My father, answering sharply and proudly, told her, 'Madam, all my sons have enlisted and all are volunteers.'

Father would have liked to join up himself, but he was too old even to falsify his age.

Being a voluntary enlistment, I was allowed to select my

regiment, and I elected to join the Royal Fusiliers Public Schools Brigade. Another OTC boy, Ronnie, had done the same as myself, and within a few days we were off to Oxford where the reserve battalion was stationed. Thus our quiet, close-knit family, which had been disturbed only by rare squabbles, was split, and it never came together again as such. My three sisters, Edith, Eleanor and Jennie suffered most from the war, although they stayed at home and were forbidden to join any women's wartime occupation. All three lost young men who might have been their husbands if they had not died, at St Julien, Loos and on the Somme. One of the saddest results of the first great war was that many, many maidens were condemned to remain as such for the rest of their lives as their lovers had been killed; they were left only a few relics, one or two letters, and a little headstone engraved with a regimental badge in a military cemetery.

The first sight of Oxford was exciting and refreshing for Ronnie and me; it was so totally different from dirty industrial Newcastle. At that time it was still a small university and market town. In peacetime the majority of the townspeople gained their livings directly or indirectly from the colleges; but now nearly all the undergraduates and many of the staff had departed for the war and the tradesmen and landladies were suffering. It was perhaps for this reason that four battalions originally made up of university and public school boys were stationed there in billets.

After reporting for duty at Battalion HQ, Ronnie and I were conducted to a lodging house behind Ruskin College, which was kept by a frail, crippled old lady who had boarded several generations of undergraduates. She was not pleased to have eight soldiers instead, but the billeting money provided her living. Except for the corporal in charge of us, we had all come from decent homes and gave her little trouble, but she was always peevish and querulous.

Ronnie and I were given single cots in an attic room, and we settled down to sleep, tired after our journey. But not for long. Our military duties started with alarming promptitude just after midnight, when we were awakened by bugles sounding the alarm, a peculiarly expressive, unmistakable signal for immediate action—ta ta ta ti ta—ta ta ta ti ta. Our corporal rushed into the room shouting, 'Up and out'. We dressed quicker than ever before and followed him out into the streets where hundreds of soldiers were assembling at their alarm posts. We drew picks and shovels from a store and then waited shivering with cold in the cattle market for several hours, until we were dismissed to our billets. It was rumoured that a Zeppelin had been seen forty miles away, but this was never confirmed.

Next day after kitting-out, we recruits were placed in a squad to begin our basic training in drill; however, as Ronnie and I were reasonably proficient, we were soon promoted to learn our musketry.

I loved the life from the beginning, and I have never regretted joining the army or any of my service in it since. My only trial at the time was shortage of money, as my pay was seven shillings a week and I had allotted half of that to my parents. The financial position of my family at that time can be judged by the fact that my parents considered three-and-sixpence a week ample pocket money for a lad of my age, and were surprised that other parents sent money to their sons. Not wishing to sponge on my friends in the billet, I spent my off-duty hours wandering round the colleges and on the river banks; and I spent the evenings reading in a soldiers' club, which was established in a church hall and called, with surprising innocence, by the churchgoers who ran it, 'The Red Lamp'.

Oxford was a 'cushy' station, perhaps too 'cushy', as our battalion was soon hoicked out of it and entrained for Scotland. Why the War Office suddenly decided to move four battalions of English troops to garrison Edinburgh is still a mystery to me; it seemed unlikely that there was to be a rising of the clans or a German invasion up the Firth of Forth, and the citizens of Edinburgh were doubtless affronted by the sight of Sassenach soldiers on the ramparts of their castle. Perhaps High Command thought we were too comfortable in billets and decided to toughen us up in the bracing climate of North Britain.

En route I had my first experience of travelling by troop train; I remember it vividly, and as I write I can still smell sweaty soldiers. All soldiers smell *en masse*, but on the march the odour is dissipated in the open air. In a troop train, it is confined, as the majority of soldiers are afraid of draughts and prefer to live in a steamy fug. We were packed ten to a compartment in a non-corridor train, with all our kit and no toilets, and the train stopped only once during the ten-hour journey — at Carlisle, where we got a mug of tea and rushed to the latrines. As most of the men had been celebrating with quantities of beer, the windows were being used as lavatory seats most of the time, the occupants being held in place so that they did not fall out. At first it was all rather revolting to a sensitive lad like myself, but I soon became accustomed to the cruder side of soldiering. The greater part of the journey was made during the night, and eventually the soldiers fell asleep, higgledy-piggledy, snoring, sweating and belching. Being small and slim, I was able to stretch out full-length under a seat.

It was mid-morning when we detrained, half awake, at Caledonian Station. Sergeants bellowed at us to adjust our equipment and fall in in fours on the platform. Although we were only half-trained troops, our superiors were anxious that we should make a good impression on the citizens of Auld Reekie, who were assembling to see us march off through their city. We were wearing greatcoats, as our packs were stuffed with extra kit and blankets, and when I finally adjusted my harness I could hardly stand up straight. I doubted that I could march carrying so much weight and a rifle; but, curiously, I rather liked wearing full accoutrements, having in mind a quotation from Mark Twain's *A Connecticut Yankee in King Arthur's Court* — 'Armour is heavy, yet a man stands well in it!' With boyish enthusiasm I thought that carrying all this equipment made me a proper soldier at last, and pride helped me to bear the weight.

Our band led the column up the Brunsfield Road, and the soldiers leant forward under their burdens to tackle the gradient. When the order to march at ease was given, I remained at the slope, with my long Lee Enfield rifle on my shoulder and did not sling it. My right shoulder has been a trifle distorted since birth, and extra weight on it is sometimes painful; in addition, since I am short, a slung rifle impeded my legs. I must have looked particularly young and slight, for I remember a woman with a shawl over her head exclaiming, 'Just look at that puir wee laddie there — 'tis sair ootragious to tak that bairn for a sodjer,' as I marched past her.

My company marched farther than any other, up the hill to Brunsfield Elementary School, which was to be our quarters; and though it was only a couple of miles from the station, we were exhausted by the time we reached it. During the 1914 war, it was a common practice to quarter soldiers in schools, while the children were taught elsewhere, as there were few other buildings with the same facilities for sleeping and messing large numbers of men. Brunsfield School was, and probably still is, a sound stone building. It had two floors, each with an assembly hall and several classrooms which accommodated about fifty men each. However, the floors were tiered, men sleeping at different levels, and occasionally a restless sleeper would slide off his piece of floor on to the man below and start a sort of human avalanche, which only ended up against the blackboard on the wall.

By the time we had been allotted our places and tramped about, the whole building was covered with mud and rubbish. Thus, after dumping our kit, scores of us, including myself, spent hours on our knees scrubbing the floors with cold water and army soap. Within ten minutes after the job was finished it was fouled again; all soldiers, having laboured to clean a floor, will immediately walk over it in muddy boots. Thoughout my service I have not discovered the reason for this nor been able to prevent it. We slept on the floor for several nights, but we were then given straw paliasses (donkeys' breakfasts) and bed-boards with low trestles to make cots and on which we laid our kit in daytime.

I got separated from my close friends, Ronnie and Raymond, with whom I had been in the Oxford billet, and I found myself in a room with much rougher types; the new intakes into the battalion were turning it from a university and public school corps into a workhouse and public house regiment. The soldier who slept next to me had lately been released from jail and still had jail-cropped hair. He was a tough little cockney, about my height, addressed as Twig, quite illiterate but very talkative. It was distressing to hear him try to express himself with his very small vocabulary, which was made up mostly of four-letter words. To colour his conversation, he would insert them even between the syllables of words. His favourite expression was 'fuckee says I'. He would gabble off a sentence such as, 'I says to fuckee corporal when he tells me to scrub fuckee floor — what's the i-fuckee-dea? I was on fuckee fatigue yesterday — fuckee says I to him.'

Twig and I got on splendidly after a couple of days; I liked him for he had a generous nature and was never surly. We helped each other to clean and assemble our kit, and though he was naturally suspected of being a barrack-room thief, he stole nothing from me and guarded my belongings when I was absent. He was so unlearned that he looked upon me as a man of great education, and I was touched when he asked me childish questions about something he could not understand or to read something which he could not. When I answered he would exclaim, 'Blimey, Bas, fuckee says I if you ain't a fuckee scholar.'

We never had a cross word all the time we were together, but we grumbled to each other about our room corporal who was suspected of having been expelled from the police, although this was never proven. Naturally, Twig and he were at loggerheads; I escaped some of his blustering wrath by not answering back. The remainder of the men in the room had recently been called up on the Derby Scheme; they were not particularly ardent soldiers but were amenable to discipline, and we had little army crime.

We had among us an elderly Billy Bunter nicknamed 'Stug', from 'guts' spelt backwards. He was a slow-moving stolid chap in his late thirties; he had an insatiable appetite and was always first at the mess table, and last away, as he used to finish all the scraps of food he could find, including those from other men's plates. Sometimes our food was almost uneatable, but never to Stug. One day, being mess orderly, I was waiting to clear up the table, and I watched him eat sixteen kippers, the rations of sixteen men, who after one taste had declared them rotten and stinking to high heaven.

Another odd character was an absent-minded 'varsity lecturer who read Ovid through pebble spectacles and spoke in quotations from Shakespeare and the Classics. He was a nice chap, but an appalling soldier; his bed, uniform and kit were always in a deplorable condition, and though our standard of turn-out was not high, he never approached it. He was rarely on time for any parade or fatigue, and when he was fetched he apologized so profusely and so sincerely in such impeccable English, far above the heads of the NCOs, that they were abashed and took little disciplinary action. I remember him being put on a charge only once, and being brought before the company commander, but even then his courteous excuses for his misdemeanours and for troubling his commander were so profound and so amusing that he was let off with a caution; when he was marched out the officers present exploded in gales of laughter. Eventually, he became a company butt and pet, and his superiors were amazingly tolerant of him. He was always polite to everyone and there was no harm in him. His services could have been used to better advantage in the war. He could never have been turned into a soldier, but, poor fellow, he died a soldier's death on the Somme.

All of our few officers had done a spell at the front, and some were convalescing after wounds; we saw little of them, most of the training being carried out by NCOs. Training for static trench warfare was simple, and we trained for nothing else, never going on sham fights or manoeuvres. It required little intelligence, and consisted mainly of a little desultory squad and arms drill and some musketry, which was the word used then for weapon training. We fired a course with live ammunition on a range at Arthur's Seat, the saddle-shaped hill overlooking Edinburgh; and then practised rapid fire at faintly illuminated targets at night, when the results were rather better than those in daylight. We used our long Lee Enfield rifles and some Japanese types, but we never fired with the short Lee Enfield used at the front. The most valuable part of our training for war was marching, and we marched at least a dozen miles a day in full kit, up the Braid Hills, where we practised trench digging and grenade throwing. We progressed from bags of sand simulating Mills grenades to live hand bombs thrown from a sandbag enclosure on to a target, and as I threw better than the average, I was put on a course with a dozen others and qualified as something they called a Special Bomber. Looking back, I am horrified at the hazards we took assembling, stripping and detonating all types of grenades, tried and untried, some of which were highly dangerous. I could not be so oblivious of the consequences now. I handle firearms with great respect, remembering the remark of a CSM of mine to careless recruits, 'I'm not frightened of loaded bondooks (rifles) — it's the unloaded ones that shoot you.'

At the end of the course, I was awarded a red and gilt badge in the form of a bursting grenade to wear on my sleeve — the first insignia for which I qualified. I was enormously chuffed by it.

During the summer of 1916, the Allied offensive battles on the Somme resulted in dreadful and unexpected casualties, and our reserve battalion was called upon for drafts to make up those decimated by the few days' fighting. All my intake of recruits and many men with even less service and training were detailed, and we were sent immediately to have our heads shorn. The barber imported for the purpose simply ran his clippers as close to the skin as possible and finished his work, standing in six inches of hair, in an astonishingly short time; we all roared with laughter at the sight of sixty-odd bald-headed men together in one room. In this hirsute age, when even soldiers are allowed hair of immoderate length, it is necessary to explain that this was done as a prophylactic measure against head lice, and although it was not compulsory, shaving of other body hair was recommended for the same purpose.

We were then sent on draft leave, and our appearance must have shocked our relatives. As soon as my family saw me they knew that I was going to the front, there was no need to tell them. It was an unhappy furlough, and I was glad to return to Edinburgh to meet my friends again. Raymond, our rich ranker, had rented a couple of rooms shortly after our arrival in Edinburgh, in a suburb not far from our quarters. They provided a refuge from the hurly-burly of the barrack rooms and the coarseness and never-ending swearing amongst the troops. He was a religious man but by no means bigoted or a proselyte, and he provided hospitality for those who would appreciate peace and quiet and a properly-cooked meal provided by his landlady. A few drinks were provided for guests, even though he himself was very abstemious, and he taught several of us to play bridge, which was then becoming fashionable, although he would not play for money. I also learned why many men of the upper classes were leaders and automatically took command over others: four of us spent the evening before our departure for the front in these rooms, a welcome escape from the many men in the school who were having their last drunken fling before being sent into the inferno of the Western Front. I asked Raymond why he had joined the ranks, as he was first-class officer material; and for the first time I learned that he was a Plymouth Brother, who might have claimed exemption from combatant duties even if he had been called up. He said that at first he was a pacifist, but a growing awareness of German atrocities had forced him to the conclusion that the Germans could be stopped only by force. As he was a big, strong man he thought it his duty to volunteer — he did not wish to be a pressed man — and more-over, to experience the privations of men in the ranks so that he would be better able to lead them if eventually commissioned. I never heard him grouse or complain about a stupid order from some moronic NCO; and although at first he was looked upon as a 'softy', very soon he was respected and slightly feared by most men and some non-commissioned ranks, and his presence and a few quiet words could stop any barrack-room squabble.

None of us thought we were going to a picnic, as did the first of the new armies, and there was not much joking or even excitement in the barrack room as we put our kit together for the last time in Edinburgh; few of us slept well that night. Next morning, after a hasty breakfast, we paraded in the school yard and were given sandwiches for the journey. As I was handed mine the CSM barked at me, 'Peacock, you are reserve man; you are under age, but if any man is missing when we reach the station, you will go with the draft.'

There was one man missing from parade — our university lecturer — and this caused some commotion, as it was thought he had jumped the draft and deserted. A search party was sent through the building and in a few minutes the missing man appeared, his full marching order hanging about him like parcels on a Christmas tree. He held a small book in one hand and his rifle in the other, and trotted up to the draft conducting officer, gave him a slight bow and said, 'I much regret to have kept you all waiting. Thinking I had half an hour to spare, I thought it advisable to visit the toilets and became so interested in this book of verse that time passed without my knowledge. My apologies to you, sir.'

Everyone, including the officer, roared with laughter; the CSM was so relieved that he had a full muster, he simply called him a bloody fool and told him to fall in the ranks. The incident relieved the strain that most of us were feeling. The colonel appeared with his adjutant and inspected us casually, but he said little except to wish us good luck in our new units. By this time in the war most people had given up patriotic speeches and jingoism, and I had the impression that the two officers were sad to see us depart; they had no illusions about the war in France.

The band played us to Waverley Station; this helped us along, we were heavily laden and the few folk in the streets just stared at us dourly. It may have been that they did not approve of our band, it was a Sunday and military music was not thought fitting on the Sabbath, although bagpipes were. A special train was waiting and the draft entrained with little fuss; but I was told to stand aside on the platform. I managed a few final words with Ronnie and Raymond before the train pulled out; I waved as it slid away and they passed out of my life. I was nearly in tears; I felt like a deserter and was not cheered by the CSM roughly ordering me to walk back to barracks, telling me, 'The CO has had a letter from your parents telling him you are just eighteen—too young for France. He will be wanting to see you in the orderly room'.

He never did and did not remark on my having falsified my age until some months later.

The school looked desolate when I returned, and for a few days there were only three of us in the room, the other two being under medical treatment. We were all very depressed; but, unknown to us, we were fortunate indeed as hardly a man of that draft survived more than a few weeks.

Within a fortnight, I received a letter from Raymond in which he wrote, 'Remain where you are as long as possible, this is no place for you. It is hell on earth and our casualties are heavy. Ronnie agrees.'

That was the last I heard from them, and soon I learned from their relatives that they had both been killed in action. Later a survivor told me that Raymond, the one-time pacifist, met his death clearing a strip of trench at bayonet-point and should have received a posthumous decoration. In the short time he served in France, he made a name for himself as a courageous soldier, and his death was much regretted by his comrades.

Our battalion soon filled up with new intakes and with men who had been wounded and were now recovered; these poor chaps were hurriedly being retrained to be sent abroad again. I spent weeks on fatigue duties, the most loathesome of which was washer-up in the sergeants' mess, where owing to a shortage of hot water, we dunked piles of greasy plates in a sort of brown soup and dried them with filthy towels. It is difficult to understand why there was no outbreak of food poisoning. I did not hold this job long before I was promoted to the cookhouse. This was located under the school shed in the playground, and the equipment consisted of a few boilers in fireplaces and several cast-iron ovens heated by coal. Two extra wooden huts had been run up to serve as bread store and butchers' shop; both were rat-infested and any loaves of bread left in the store overnight were eaten through by morning. The so-called cooks were some of the stupidest and dirtiest men in the company, and they were presumably given this job because they were unfit for anything else. I doubt if any of them had trained as cooks; only the butcher had done the same job in civilian life. Like many cooks, they drank a great deal; one in particular was a womanizer, he thought of little else, and he eventually contracted VD. They were some of the roughest men I ever met in my service; but I must state that although I was occasionally teased, I was never bullied by them and was often treated with kindness. A cheerful but stupid corporal was in charge, and under his slapdash directions we served up horrible meals and spoiled a great deal of good rations. There was practically no supervision of the mess-ing; the cookhouse itself was inspected only cursorily by the orderly officer on Saturdays, and the staff for this one day in the week turned out in clean white overalls. The remainder of the time we looked like ship's greasers or chimney sweeps. We had few cooking utensils or cleaning materials, our stiff yard-broom was often used to scrub potatoes. There were rarely any fatigue men to peel them, so they were served in their jackets boiled or roasted, and the soldiers removed the skins at their mess tables. We had an enormous tin bath in which one of the cooks, supposedly the baker, made plum duff or pie-crust. I occasionally helped him, putting my arms up to my elbows in flour and water; it was preferable to my usual job of cleaning out boilers and attending to fires. I was excused one fatigue — that of carrying carcasses from the ration wagon to the butchers' shop, because the first time a fore-quarter of beef was put on my shoulder, I collapsed under it and was pinned down by its weight; I could not move until the corporal and butcher, roaring with laughter, lifted it off me. The corporal rarely appeared till after breakfast, and he detailed two cooks in turn to cook this meal. Sometimes the second man did not turn up, and I reached the peak of my culinary career when I made the tea and porridge, and broiled three hundred kippers in their own grease, to feed the rest of the company. I could not stand the smell of kippers for months afterwards.

If roast meat was intended for dinners, the men rarely got it, as it was seldom cooked in time. About half an hour before cookhouse bugle-call the corporal would realize that the meat was still half-raw, and all hands would set about carving it into lumps which were fried in their own fat in large mess tins. No soldier would tolerate this sort of food nowadays, and I used to speculate what I should do if instead of muttering and grousing the men took militant action against the cookhouse staff. The nearest they came to this was when we served up rice as a vegetable because of a shortage of potatoes.

Fortunately, before everybody was poisoned, a real sergeant cook arrived. He took one look at the cookhouse and went berserk: on lifting up the lid of something we called a stockpot he discovered several gallons of sludge crawling with maggots, and in the bread store fifty stale loaves eaten through with vermin. He immediately put the corporal and two others on a charge. I escaped because by chance I had just washed myself and changed my overalls, which had got particularly foul that morning. He remarked that the only person who seemed to know anything about hygiene was the bloody boy. Within a few days, and with different cooks, he had transformed our messing, until, although still a bit rough, the food was eatable.

Shortly afterwards, I was told to report to the company office in clean white overalls. 'I don't think you like the cookhouse, do you, Peacock?' said the captain when I was marched in front of him. 'You would rather be on parade and I think you might make a Lewis gunner. You may leave the cookhouse any time if you wish.'

'I would like to go now, sir,' I replied with enthusiasm.

He smiled, said, 'Arrange that, sergeant-major,' and continued, 'You were once an OTC boy, were you not? You know you can be accepted for officer training at eighteen. Think about it.'

The CSM marched me out and barked, 'Hand in those

1. The author, 1912, aged fourteen, as a schoolboy at Rutherford College, Newcastle-upon-Tyne.

2. Uncle Archie, *circa* 1880, when serving in India with the 17th Lancers.

3. The Peacock family in 1899 – left to right, Alex, Mother, the author, Jim, Jennie, Eleanor, Father, Edith.

ALEC   BASIL   JIM

RAMC   UNIV OTC   PUBLIC SCHOOLS BN
                                       ROYAL FUSILEERS.

4. Soldiers Three, 1915: Alex, RAMC; Basil, OTC; Jim, Royal
Fusiliers.
5. The Cooks, Royal Fusiliers; Edinburgh, 1916; the author is
seated on the ground.

6. As a private in the Royal Fusiliers, 1916.

7. As a Second Lieutenant in the 3rd Battalion, the Northumberland Fusiliers, 1917.

Four stages in the author's military career.

8. As a Major in the Territorial Army, 1939.

9. On his return from the Far East, 1945.

10. Officers of the 32nd Coy, 31st S/L Bn. RE, 1934.

11. 14 S/L Battery Royal Artillery, Changi, Singapore, 1941.

overalls and tidy up your bloody bed. You lousy cooks have the worse kit lay-out in the company.'

I hurried away, delighted. I joined a squad learning to use the Lewis gun which had newly arrived in our battalion; owing to scarcity this type of weapon was normally used only at the front. I learned a lot about that particular gun, and even during the Second World War I could handle, strip, and assemble one better than most of my NCOs.

Taking up my captain's suggestion I set about obtaining the necessary papers and applied for a commission. The company commander referred me to the colonel, and I spent a long time polishing my buttons, badges and boots for the interview.

'This is Peacock, sir,' said the adjutant, 'one of those A4 boys (under age personnel) applicant for officer training.'

'Good God,' exclaimed the colonel, 'he's starting young. How old are you, boy?'

I told him and he asked the adjutant if he had checked my birth certificate. 'Right then; they keep asking us for candidates. Send him to see the brigadier. He still looks damn young to me. Good luck, boy.'

I saluted and was marched out. The interview with the brigadier was even shorter. He signed the papers, only glancing up to remark on my youthful appearance, and said, 'I am recommending you for an officer cadet battalion.'

So that was that. All I had to do now was to wait and to behave myself for a few weeks. I could do little else; I could afford no vices except two cigarettes a day, as I spent the remainder of my three-and-sixpence per week on extra food, as I was always hungry in the evenings. Instead of attending the nearest soldiers' club, I used to walk two miles to another because the price of a plate of porridge there was one penny instead of two. I could not afford a half-fare voucher to visit home on week-end leave unless my parents sent me money. One week I was in funds having been paid 'pig-swill money' during my spell in the cook-house: pig breeders bought swill from us and this money was considered cooks' perks, and I received the handsome sum of thirty-six shillings. Most of this was stolen from a money belt which I carelessly left lying about for a few minutes, but I still had seven-and-six. This I expended on seeing five Gilbert and Sullivan operas in one week from the gallery of the Lyric Theatre, one shilling entrance money.

Being so penurious, I could not afford the company of girls; thus, I cannot write of an exciting sex life as is depicted in modern books about virgin soldiers. I can recall only a bit of canoodling on a sofa with a romantic flapper (her parents had asked me to visit their home as a kindness to a lonely soldier), and an unsatisfactory walk up the Braid Hills with a forward young piece who thought I was a bit slow.

Since I was considered to be a trained soldier, I 'copped a lot of guards' and spent many hours on sentry go. There were several sentry-beats in Edinburgh Castle; I preferred the main gate as this was not as lonely as the rest. The flagstones at the gate were rutted six inches deep by the constant tramp of sentinels over the centuries, and there were deep cavities in the walls where the points of bayonets had eroded the stones as the soldiers turned about. The worst sentry-beat was one nearly at the top of the castle, bitterly cold even in midsummer and supposedly haunted. It was called the Jewel Guard and at two o'clock in the morning, it was very spooky; once in fright I nearly shot a cat. It is said that sentries have occasionally been found dead at this post, and I quite believe it—they were probably frozen to death. Friday and Saturday nights were busy times for the guard, as the military police used to carry in the drunks, mostly Jocks in kilts, who had been creating disturbances. They were generally fighting drunk, and with Scottish fervour they objected to 'the fucking Sassenachs in oor fucking castle!' Four of the guards would pin them down, removed their boots and belts, and thrust them down some stone steps into a sort of dungeon to cool off. They soon got tired of trying to kick the door down with stockinged feet and fell into a drunken sleep. By morning they were properly cooled off because the dungeons were like ice boxes, and they were grateful for the cup of cocoa we gave them when they awoke.

One of my last guards was at battalion headquarters; on that occasion I was the 'stick man', which meant I was supposedly the best turned out soldier and was being rewarded by having simple duties and being excused sentry-go. On this occasion, the RSM bellowed from his office for the 'stick man'; when I reported he handed me a mess tin and some money and told me to buy beer. I returned with the full tin and twopence change; nodding to the RQMS he said to me nobly, 'Keep the change, boy, you haven't taken a drop.'

Four months later, I returned in officer's uniform to visit the adjutant, and the same RSM, a giant of a man, sprang to attention, gave me the most explosive salute I have ever received and bellowed at the sentry nearby, 'Officer passing, let me hear you slap that butt of your rifle.'

I never knew whether he recognized me or not.

Orders came for me to report to Cambridge No. 2 Officer Cadet Battalion. I was given a new uniform by the CQMS and received a handshake from the CSM, who asked me to write to him about the training since he thought he might apply for a commission himself. Oddly, I did meet him, wearing brand new pips, on the Western Front the following year and was able to give him some help in finding his unit.

I had learned much in the ranks, enough to excuse soldiers' foibles when I came to command some; I had also become convinced that the majority will respond better to a word of encouragement than to denigration. I am certain that a prospective officer should not spend too long in the ranks, for if he does he may become so accustomed to waiting for orders that he loses his initiative in giving them, or become a martinet to bolster his ego. However, I do think that all officers should have experience in a cookhouse and on sentry-go; these duties are much more arduous than the average officer is aware of. In the cookhouse he will learn something of hygiene, and on sentry-go that two hours on a post in the middle of the night can seem interminable and that even the most willing of soldiers may unintentionally fall asleep. I could keep awake only by repeating such verses of poetry as I could remember.

I had a couple of days at home *en route* for Cambridge, and my parents were at last convinced that I was enjoying myself. Mother and my sisters were more interested in my adventures in the cookhouse than in anything else, and they were highly amused to hear that when we occasionally boiled plum duff in pieces of khaki shirts the pudding was dyed coffee-coloured.

I left Newcastle Central Station, the starting point for my travels to many strange places and odd experiences throughout the world, with less than a pound in my pocket and no field-marshal's baton in my haversack, *en train* for Cambridge.

Chapter 3

THE FLEDGLING OFFICERS

THE Cambridge colleges, almost denuded of undergraduates, now housed the personnel of two officer cadet battalions. The officers, some of them dons of the 'varsity, lived in dons' quarters, and the cadets occupied the undergraduates' rooms. In Corpus Christi the college staff were still there, doing their normal jobs of portering, cooking, waiting, and the old lady 'bedders' tidied our rooms and saw to our washing. I shared a room in New Quad with another young cadet, who, sad to say, was killed in France only a week or so after he was commissioned. We were encouraged to live the lives of undergraduates, but studying military subjects instead of those in the normal curriculum.

Our course lasted three months. At first we drilled a great deal; we then attended lectures on tactics, military law, map-reading, and some field engineering, none of which was very abstruse. We took turns in acting as sergeants and platoon commanders; a great deal of the instruction was directed to turning us into instructors. We were encouraged to take part in games; I became a scrum-half for the company rugby team and, being jumped on by loose forwards twice a week suffered the bruising of players in that position. There was a boxing competition in which I outpointed two opponents who had no idea of the sport and then received the biggest hiding of my life in the final from one who did. He said cheerfully in the dressing-room afterwards, 'I was trying to knock you out properly, Basil. Pity your seconds threw the towel in just before the end of the third round.'

I said that I was so dazed that I wouldn't have known if he had knocked me out.

At the end of the term we were given an examination and tested in our ability as instructors. I was ordered to detail the drill for piling arms, which seemed a fairly useless military procedure in trench warfare. During our written examination, an officer invigilator leaned over my shoulder and remarked, 'You've got your dispositions of a company marked on the map quite reasonably but your "fines for drunkenness" are all to cock are they not—nothing for the first offence, 2/6 for the second, 5/- for the third and 7/6 to 10/- subsequently?'

I doubt if the final examinations counted for much: the cadets were assessed throughout the course, and unlikely candidates were returned to their units after the first week or two.

Before the examination results were published, we had a ceremonial parade on top of the Gog and Magog hills. After some battalion drill, we were drawn up for inspection by His Royal Highness, The Duke of Connaught, who knew more about the army than many high-ranking generals. It was a bitterly cold day and Cambridge district can be one of the coldest in England. We stood to attention awaiting the great man, getting colder and colder; I could feel that my nose was bright blue and that tears were running down my cheeks. His Highness walked slowly down the line of frozen cadets, and, probably alarmed at the sight of me, the smallest, youngest and coldest one in the front rank, stopped and said, 'Are you feeling unwell, boy? I must say you are standing to attention correctly and still.'

I could not have done otherwise as I felt like an upright icicle. 'Where do you come from?' he continued, 'and what regiment do you hope to join if commissioned?'

My lips were almost frozen together but I managed to stammer, 'Newcastle, sir, and I hope to join the Northumberland Fusiliers.'

'Ah,' replied the great man, 'you mean the Old Fifth; now there's a first-class regiment for you. Make sure you are a credit to it.'

He passed along the line leaving me warmed and bursting with pride, for myself as the only cadet in the front rank whom he spoke to, and for his comments on our county regiment.

During our course we had been measured and fitted with officers' service dress with a white band round our caps, and we wore the belt of the Sam Browne harness. After the examination we were told we could go on leave wearing our uniforms but that we might have to return for extra training if our results were poor. I was still hard up, and as we were given only half-fare travel warrants, I decided to wait for the examination results before leaving, since I could not afford two journeys. After two days spent hanging about, our sports officer and rugger coach caught sight of me and asked why I had not gone on leave. Shamefacedly, I explained. 'Good heavens, lad,' he exclaimed, laughing, 'I think I can guess that you have passed and will have a pip on your shoulder after a few days.'

He winked and continued, 'Now, off with you on leave and good luck.'

I saluted, thanked him, and ran back to my quarters where I found a letter from my parents waiting for me enclosing some money — enough for the fare and a bit over.

Father was proud to see me in officer's clothes, and he could now tell his customers that all his sons had been promoted to commissioned rank. Mother admitted that I looked more respectable, but any military uniform was still anathema to her. After a few days, I received official notice from the War Office appointing me a second lieutenant (Special Reserve) in The Northumberland Fusiliers and directing me to report to the depot at East Boldon, County Durham. Sister Edith sewed a cloth star on each of my shoulder straps, and I assumed the cross strap of my Sam Browne belt. I was a commissioned officer at last, and, feeling very puffed up, I started off to the city to celebrate. Within a few hundred yards of home, a private soldier passed me and saluted. I called him back and whispered that I was newly fledged and would he care to accept half a crown to drink my health and wish me luck. Years after the war, the same man stopped me in the street and reminded me of the incident. Having a bit more sense then, I apologized thinking he had been insulted. He laughed, and replied, 'Good Lord, half a crown was a devil of a lot of money in those days; and besides, I recognized you, though you did not recognize me; we were in infant school together.'

The depot at East Boldon was like most depots at the time — crowded with officers and men, too many to train properly, all waiting for postings to the various fronts. The officers were a mixed bag, a few regulars on administrative duties; some tough temporary ones who had seen active service and were making the most of their short remission from the trenches, drinking and wenching if possible; and the remainder were newly fledged like myself. We youngsters were skilfully cheated by some of the depot staff, paying unnecessary subscriptions to this and that fund which we were told was obligatory for officers on appointment. The rapid turnover of personnel in the depot, which was serving 52 battalions of the regiment, was too speedy for complaints to be redressed or even submitted, as most individuals were on draft within a few days.

Within a fortnight, I was detailed and was on my way to Folkestone to a transit camp for the Western Front. Again, I began a journey from Newcastle Central Station; this time I was off to my first war. It was a few days after my nineteenth birthday.

Chapter 4

OFF TO THE WARS

AFTER one night in an old warehouse at Folkestone several hundred troops prepared to embark for France. My brother, Alex, who is twelve years older than I, came to see me off, as he was stationed near by on some special duties after two years at the front. I was still the baby brother to him, and he was obviously distraught that I was on my way to the hardships and horrors which he had already experienced. I remember tears coming into his eyes as I remarked casually, 'I suppose I should make some sort of will now I am receiving officers' pay.'

His murmured reply was, 'Oh, dear, dear, plenty of time for that, I guess.'

After the war when Alex was a professor, lecturing students on circulation of the blood, he used to introduce his talk with words similar to these:

'A statue to Doctor Harvey, the great physician, who first discovered the circulation of the blood in our bodies, stands by the side of the road leading to the quay at Folkestone. No site could be more appropriate. We might say that blood circulated round it, for tens of thousands of men marched down that road, and later were carried up it after shedding their blood in Flanders.'

I had been placed in charge of a draft of mixed details, and with the help of a sergeant I collected the soldiers and marched them down the road to embark on the old paddle-steamer *Brighton Belle*. It was a raw, drizzly day and a few on board were seasick, but I was too interested in our

escort vessels and my first view of a foreign coastline to
suffer: My first glimpse of it was an enormous advertise-
ment for Johnnie Walker's whisky on a high hoarding.
When we berthed, I walked around Boulogne which was
then an almost medieval town, with fascinating gabled
houses and narrow cobbled streets, much more attractive
then than the new one raised after its destruction in the
Second World War.

As we waited to disembark, and for baggage to be
slung ashore, some of the newcomers began to sing, 'Pack
up your troubles in your old kit bag', and others shouted,
'Are we down-hearted?' 'No.'

A very old soldier on shore, who looked as though he
had been out since Mons and with Kitchener to Khartoum
before that, paused in his task of sweeping the quay, looked
up leaning on his broom and shouted back, 'And you fucking
soon will be.' The song and shouting died away.

A train puffed up along the quay, and we disembarked and
entrained immediately to travel for the first time in cattle
trucks, bearing the sign of all French rolling stock 'Hommes
40 Chevaux 8'. With an absurd peep from the massive
engine, Chemin de Fer du Nord, we began the first of
many journeys in France, at a walking pace, along the
coast to Etaples, a small fishing village near the mouth
of the Ancre. We soon fell silent and thoughtful, for border-
ing the lines were acres and acres of graves where tens of
thousands of Commonwealth soldiers and a few Germans,
who would never return to their homes, lay in lines as
though still on parade. With the resilience of youth we
forgot about them for a time in the excitement of detraining
at the main base camp, marquees, Nissen huts, and bell
tents erected on the sandy dune-land which stretched for
miles.

I handed over my draft to a receiving officer and was
directed to an orderly room to report; thence to a bell
tent which had five other occupants, all second lieutenants,
whose sleeping valises lay on the ground round the pole.
Young subalterns were three a penny, and were treated
as such, being just passing visitors whose stay was brief.

We messed in a sort of canvas hut, at a separate table from the permanent officers sitting serene behind their medal ribbons, and we felt shy and raw.

In his poem *Base Details*, Siegfried Sassoon wrote:

'If I were fierce, and bold, and short of breath,
I'd live with scarlet majors at the base,
And speed glum heroes up the line to death.'

I think, maybe, he was overstating his case, as many of these 'scarlet majors' had already done their stint; some were not entirely fit and were entitled to a rest from the front line.

Most young officers like myself spent about ten days at the base awaiting posting to their units, and we were given some final training on what was called 'The Bull Ring'. This was an area of sand dunes on which were field works, bombing ranges, and covered trenches in which one experienced small doses of poison gas. The instructors were ancient sergeants, thankful that if their luck held their fighting days were over. To remain in their cushy jobs they did a great deal of shouting and verbal bullying of junior ranks, making a show of keenness and efficiency when within earshot of the camp staff. For the same reason, they were not too respectful to young officers, but out of earshot of 'scarlet majors' they were only too anxious to slack off and have a quiet smoke. Some may have been scrimshankers, but most were just prematurely-aged men from regular units. One elderly, dour, kilted Jock with bushy eyebrows used to start his lectures on gas warfare by looking fixedly at the subalterns for a few moments, then announcing, 'Gentlemen, it is my ordered duty to teach ye something about poison gas'; he would then pause, shake his head and continue, 'but I'm thinking — what's the use — as most of ye will be mouldering under the sod in aboot a fortnight.'

The base and The Bull Ring were depressing places, and I was glad to be on my way to join the 22nd Battalion The Northumberland Fusiliers with two other newly commissioned officers. It took us nearly all day to travel the forty miles to Mercatel, where a driver with a limber for our baggage took us to Battalion HQ in a room in a farmhouse. The village was well back from the front line and was used as a rest area. By normal standards, the troops were comfortably housed, in barns, although they lived in a permanent odour of manure from the dung heaps adjacent to them.

The commanding officer, Acklom, who interviewed us was a pre-war regular captain of the HLI, now holding the temporary rank of lt.-colonel. He was not yet thirty and had survived many battles, including that on the Somme where, on 1st July, 1916, he was one of only three officers of the battalion left to bring out the remnants. He was very pleasant; he looked keenly at me as he queried my age and sent me to A Company. This company was then commanded by Captain Charlton, who I thought was a middle-aged man but years later discovered was only twenty-eight at the time. He was a sedate chap with charming manners, a pipe constantly in his mouth, and very soon I admired him as a fine soldier. Like the colonel, he had seen much active service; he was a temporary officer and survived the war, but he never received a decoration, though to my knowledge he deserved several. He, too, queried my age and appointed me to No. 1 Platoon, which I thought a great honour as it led the whole battalion on the march.

That night the officers had a mild debauch, having discovered some so-called champagne at three francs a bottle. I was too shy to join in and strong drink had rarely passed my lips, so I lay in my valise on the floor of our billet thinking, 'Here I am at last' and fell into a healthy sleep.

Next morning, at parade, everyone was wearing Scots bonnets and badges, and I learned that the battalion of Fusiliers was one of four raised with the supplementary title of Tyneside Scottish as a recruiting gimmick. Instead of a band we marched behind pipers in Cameronian tartan kilts, who were orderlies, transport men or quartermaster's store details when they were not piping. There were few actual Scots in the battalion, and the majority were Tynesiders or from the north-east of England. Soulsby, my sergeant, came from Blaydon (the village referred to in

'Blaydon Races'); he had been a pitman, and I was extremely fortunate to have the guidance of this fine man. Like many Tyneside men he was not big or burly, but immensely strong, though only about five feet six inches in height. He was always a little reserved when speaking to officers, but had an expressive face, and I could detect immediately if I had given an incorrect order or made a foolish decision. He never corrected me unless I consulted him which I did frequently if I thought he disapproved of my actions. Though he was neither a loud-mouthed NCO nor a martinet, the men obeyed him promptly without question. Looking back on those times, I have wondered why youngsters such as myself were commissioned to lead grown men. We were not particularly well trained, though we could read maps and use a compass, which, oddly enough, few of the junior ranks could then. I suppose the main duty of second lieutenants was to lead rather than direct—to lead on patrol, to be the first over the top in attack, and, if possible, to set an example to others. For this reason, the lives of most subalterns were brief, shorter than those of any other rank. Many of us, scared stiff at times, could screw up our courage to take the lead only because we knew the men were watching us, knowing this was our job. When a new officer proved himself in this way, the men were extraordinarily loyal, and he might find they were looking after him. Once, waiting in the dark to go out into 'No Man's Land', I overheard my platoon sergeant say to two men known as 'Smash' and 'Geordie', experienced toughs, 'Ye two—mind ye look after wor little platoon officer.'

They replied, 'Ye're reet theor sergeant—we'll keep close by the little bugger aal the time.'

My first introduction to actual warfare was when our battalion took over a curious part of the front line from an Indian cavalry regiment, temporarily unhorsed. It was a dark night and we could see little of the troopers except their bright eyes shining in the faint light. The officers were white, rather casual, and much cleaner and better dressed than ourselves. They had a sort of panache about them, and one expected they would start their polo again at the first opportunity. Captain Charlton, with me in attendance, took over the company headquarters dug-out, which was sunk only half-way in the ground and was roofed with curved corrugated iron. The cavalry squadron leader offered us whisky and chatted amiably about nothing in particular, and when a subadar-major standing perfectly at attention outside saluted and reported relief complete, he gathered up his map case and said, '*Tik Hai*,' and departed into the night.

When dawn came, Captain Charlton was very concerned by the sketchy field works occupied by the company. Headquarters dug-out was immediately behind the ruined village of Vileret with three platoons in unconnected posts in front of it, but there was only one communication trench through the buildings. So he immediately gave orders that there must be no movement in daytime, although the enemy was very quiet. He was right as usual, for during the afternoon a German shell screamed towards us and went clean through the curved roof of our HQ dug-out, passed over my head as I lay resting, missed by inches our cook who lay on the opposite side, penetrated the far wall and buried itself in the ground, where we found it when we fled outside. Luckily, it was a dud and did not explode, and when Captain Charlton, who had been some yards away, came running up he found me looking at it and laughing hysterically. He told me sharply to shut up! This was my baptism by fire, which, if the shell had exploded, would also have been my demise. I was lucky, and my luck held, for the very next day, having been sent with a message to a forward post, I was making my way back down the communication trench when I noticed a gooseberry bush growing some yards away. Forgetting orders, I hopped out of that trench and was filling my pockets with fruit when several shells whistled overhead and exploded twenty yards or so ahead. They all fell into the trench, and there is little doubt that if I had not climbed out of it, I would not be writing these memoirs. Everyone narrowly escaped death or wounding from time to time, and I have quoted the above incidents to illustrate that good luck was the best armour for anyone on the Western Front. The common saying at the time was, 'If your number's on a shell or bullet you will cop it whatever you do.'

During that first tour in the line another incident occurred. I was sent up with my platoon to a forward post commanded by a sergeant, to help with sandbagging the parapet and parados. The sergeant was inexperienced, having lately come from Britain and, peering over the top of the trench in the dark, saw or thought he saw a large party of Germans approaching. He was probably mistaken, but at night one could imagine all sorts of things and even the barbed wire seemed to move. He must have been jumpy, and without asking me he put up an SOS rocket, a firework emitting red and white flares. Such an SOS was a call for artillery fire and most of the guns of the division opened up, firing on prearranged lines in front of the post and frightening us out of our wits, particularly because some shells landed behind us and nearly in our trench. As we crouched down, shaking, I remembered an order I had read casually a few days before, indicating that the signal to lengthen range was two white flares fired in quick succession. The sergeant in charge of the post was nowhere to be seen but Sergeant Soulsby and I managed to find Verey pistols and cartridges and lying on our backs fired them in the air. The German guns now opened up and fired in front of us, probably thinking we were raiding, and increased the racket going on. To our relief, our guns did lengthen range, and then ceased firing, so that we were able to return to company HQ. There I found a message waiting for me to report to the colonel. When I reached his HQ, there was a gunner colonel with him, agog for explanations. 'Do you realize, boy,' said Colonel Acklom, 'that you have been responsible for expending hundreds of valuable shells costing a hell of a lot of money.'

I explained I had only put up the lengthening range signal, which he was surprised to hear I knew. The gunner colonel was niggled when I said that his guns had fired on us and asked if I was not romancing — could I not be mistaken? I offered the evidence of my experienced platoon sergeant, and Colonel Acklom came to my support, remarking testily to the gunner, 'You were several miles back and Peacock and his sergeant were on the bloody spot so I am inclined to believe them.'

There was some discussion about atmospheric conditions affecting the accuracy of guns and American-made ammunition, and then I was dismissed.

Such was my introduction to trench warfare.

Chapter 5

ALARMS AND EXCURSIONS

THOUGH luck played a great part in surviving on the Western Front, some of the older soldiers seemed to have a special genius for staying alive and whole. It is remarkable that new arrivals were often casualties, but that time after time, when formations were paraded after actions, the old soldiers stood unhurt in the ranks while the recruits were missing.

Most youngsters, especially brand-new officers, had for a time the courage of ignorance; but as this declined with experience, commanding officers sometimes used the young for risky enterprises before they lost their enthusiasm. Like most others of my age, I was at first full of zeal; because I had not seen the dire effects of active service I thought it romantic, but within a few months I was as disenchanted as the rest. I looked more like a Boy Scout than a commissioned officer; I believe it was for this reason that I was detailed for more than my share of patrol duties, and at first I preferred this to sitting getting bored in muddy trenches.

No Man's Land, the ground between the opposing front lines, was British according to our absent generals, so we spent our nights wandering about it, usually to no purpose. The Germans rarely patrolled, except in strength and then for a definite object, and sensibly sat in their comfortable, well-built dug-outs, leaving only one or two sentries on top to fire occasional shots and flares. We employed two sorts of patrols, one of three to six men for listening and reconnaissance, and a fighting patrol of about twenty men and an officer. I rarely received precise orders for the objectives of the patrols I led, except to listen, or if possible take a prisoner. It was extremely difficult to catch one, as there were few loose Germans about. They came in large parties to erect barbed wire, and they made a good job of it as their entanglements were sometimes colossal and yards deep. So to obtain a prisoner it was usually necessary to enter an enemy trench and pick up a solitary sentry, a hazardous enterprise at any time. Most patrols simply went out into No Man's Land, roamed about a little trying to be as quiet as possible, and took up positions in shell-holes freezing like statues if flares were fired by either side. During many patrols lasting several hours we got little information of any use; we might hear Fritz shouting to Hans, but as none of us knew German their remarks were meaningless, although we guessed one was telling the other his dinner was ready.

We opened fire only once, on what appeared to be a large wiring party, and heard some startled cries before several machine-guns raked our shell holes and decided us never again to give away our presence on patrol.

Once my platoon was detailed for an enterprise which might have turned out to be more exciting and dangerous than it actually was. After the battle of Cambrai, High Command suspected that the Germans would retire from a small salient which had been formed on their right flank, to shorten and tidy up their lines; and patrols were detailed to investigate. The colonel himself gave me instructions to cut through the enemy wire, lie in wait on top of the German trenches and jump on any sentry who came along. He finished by handing me a bullet-proof vest, and when I demurred about wearing it because of its weight and because the men were not to be similarly equipped, he snapped, 'It's not your life I'm thinking about; it's your utility to my battalion.'

My company officers wished us good luck, a little too heartily I thought, and with our faces blacked with soot we climbed over the top of our firing trench and unrolling a tape behind us made our way towards the German wire. It took some time to cut through it, but eventually we got through; we lay on the enemy parapet for a couple of hours getting damper and colder, until we could hardly tolerate the inactivity. I think one or two of the men went to sleep. All was deathly quiet, not a flare to be seen or a shot to be heard, and no German game about. As dawn was breaking, we returned empty-handed, disappointed, but relieved to be still alive.

'Where's the prisoner, Peacock?' said the colonel.

He disbelieved my report of a dearth of Germans, and questioned my sergeant separately, asking him to show on a map where we had been. Fortunately, he put his finger on the right place, and the colonel exclaimed, 'They must have gone — we'll send out a small party to check.'

Just then, the adjutant received a report that flares were going up from the German lines, so it was decided that the Boche were still there.

Life on the Western Front has been so vividly described, by poets and eminent literary men in innumerable books, that I feel it unnecessary to add to the bibliography of this subject, except, as this is my autobiography, to give a plain man's account of two actions, the first of which was the first attack in which I took part and the second a defeat which was not to be the last in my life.

By this time I was becoming familiar with trench warfare and reconnaissance; and I was getting a bit cocky, having escaped being wounded or even seeing anything more dreadful than an occasional casualty; but in September 1917 I had all the cockiness knocked out of me in a real battle.

Our brigade was in a comparatively quiet part of the line near Hargicourt, and the Boche seemed content to keep it so on the principle of live and let live. Unfortunately, our generals were not so pacifically inclined but persistently exhorted the troops to assume an offensive spirit. At about this time a cartoon appeared in a regimental magazine showing a foul-looking temporary gentleman (second lieutenant), with a long cigarette holder and purple socks, above the caption: 'Am I as offensive as I might be?' This was a lampoon of an official circular, which stated that every officer and man should ask himself this question.

The German lines on this part of the front ran along a low ridge which gave them an excellent opportunity to observe our dispositions, but there was no evidence that they would use the information to make an attack. Since 1915 the Germans had seldom attacked except in a properly staged large offensive with some important objective.

However, our High Command could not allow the enemy such an advantage and decided to clear the ridge, which was duly achieved. I doubt that such a trifling piece of ground was worth the lives of scores of men and the total of four hundred casualties of this battle; but the official history says these were not excessive!

Our battalion was not engaged in the preliminaries or in the first attacks but was eventually used to capture and consolidate the remaining two hundred yards of enemy trench. To do this it was necessary to dig a jumping-off trench in front of our position, and on the night of 9th September two companies including mine were sent forward to do this. We had dug down about two-and-a-half feet, making a straight ditch, when the Germans, hearing our activities, fired an intensive and accurate artillery bombardment on top of us. Although I had often experienced desultory shelling before, this was my first experience of a bombardment, and it was terrifying. We skulked in the shallow trench, trying to deepen it, and some men hacked narrow slits in the sides to gain extra protection, as the shells fell thick and close, bursting with vicious explosions and emitting the acrid stink of high explosive. Curiously, in addition to terror, the bombardment induced a slight exhilaration such as is sometimes felt in the first drenching rain of a thunderstorm, probably caused by additional adrenalin being pumped into the veins. I felt slightly intoxicated and wanted to shout aloud, but the feeling soon passed and gave place to deep fear and profound weariness. I had pushed my right shoulder and body into a newly dug slit when I noticed a soldier looking at me in disdain, and I realized that he had dug it and relinquished it to him. A moment later a shell fell on top of us knocking all the breath out of my body, and I thought I was badly hit. The soldier in the slit and another leaning against me were both killed, and several others were wounded. As I lay half-stunned, I heard the cry for stretcher-bearers, and then the anxious voice of Captain Atkinson saying gently, 'Pip (his nickname for me), where are you hit?'

I was just able to say, 'I don't know yet.'

I had blood on me from other casualties but eventually discovered that I was only winded. 'Thank God,' said Atkinson, 'I had a message you were killed.'

Having been at the front since 1915 and twice seriously wounded, he badly needed a rest. He survived the war, but is now dead. I still treasure the memory of his coming over the open during that bombardment in his concern for his boy officer.

Further operations were called off for that night, and we dribbled back to our reserve line. Atkinson looked entirely done in, and I think was partly shell-shocked, so I made my way to Battalion HQ to make a report. I remember swaying on my feet while talking to the colonel and someone saying, 'a proper balls up', and the next thing I remember was waking up hours later on the adjutant's bunk to be told I had flaked out after reporting.

Two nights later the attack was on, and we formed up in the open on a taped line in silence, champing pieces of chewing gum with which we had been issued. My platoon had been detailed to carry barbed wire and screw pickets to erect an entanglement in front of the new position when captured. I have never understood why we were not detected, we made a great deal of noise getting on to the start line carrying these in addition to our arms and equipment. The affair was to be a sudden surprise assault so there was no preliminary bombardment; but at the zero hour scores of our heavy machine-guns opened up, firing to our flanks and over our heads, and the vicious 'swish, swish' of bullets was almost more frightening than the artillery barrage which followed.

With a shout of, 'Come on the Scottish', Captain ——

(whose name I forget), led the way to the German trench. The advance was by no means a charge, for burdened as we were all we could do was to stagger over the broken ground as quickly as possible. The Germans were probably stunned by the barrage; some shots were fired at us, which were hardly noticeable in the racket going on and we gained their trench with only a few casualties. My platoon went straight over it, and Sergeant Soulsby, as ever, was the first to get to work, screwing in pickets and erecting the entanglement. We worked feverishly, anticipating a counter-attack and counter-barrage. The latter was a little slow in coming, but we were stimulated to further speed by enemy machine-guns firing at short range, and as soon as the job was done we tumbled back into the newly won trench where the other platoons were building parapets. There were a number of enemy dead lying about in contorted positions, and we took their bayonets as trophies. Everyone was in high spirits at the success we had won for such a comparatively small price, and I remember feeling intoxicated. Describing the action now, fifty-three years later, my mood is one of deep sadness, remembering the almost useless sacrifice of the fallen soldiers of both races. I may be wrong, but I still think it was an unnecessary battle since, within a few months, the Germans in a big offensive swept back across the terrain, and the British did the same in their counter-attack late in 1918.

The captain ordered me to return with my platoon to reserve trenches escorting the prisoners, about a score in all of very shaken and frightened men, and we made our way to the rear along a shallow sunken road. We were about half-way back when German guns plastered the road with heavy shells, and escort and prisoners went to earth for cover. I found myself with a German *feldwebel* (sergeant major), both of us clawing into the side of a shell-hole with our bare hands to escape the shrapnel. At one time we had our arms about each other, no longer enemies, but terrified human beings expecting death at any moment. Fortunately, the strafe was brief and we continued on our way, prisoners and escort swapping cigarettes and souvenirs, the men telling the Germans, 'San fairy ann, war na poo for you now—all OK.' (It does not matter—war finish for you. Everything is all right.)

After delivering the bag to the intelligence officer, I slept solidly for several hours in a dug-out, during which time several enemy counter-attacks were defeated by our new entanglement. Next day our battalion was relieved, and we moved back to rest. A few days later, I was playing pontoon with my company officers and holding a lucky bank, when the adjutant arrived and handed me a bit of purple and white ribbon, saying, 'You had better wear this, it's a spare piece of my own. We have just heard that you are to have a Military Cross.'

I have always felt that Sergeant Soulsby should have been the man to receive it, but military decorations do not always go to the most deserving soldiers.

Shortly after this, I contracted trench fever, a disease which was transmitted by lice. Nearly every soldier of whatever rank serving in the front lines picked up lice within a few days of his arrival, and I have always thought that this aspect of soldiering has never been given as much prominence as it should, for these pests not only transmitted fever but were a continual source of irritation, often preventing sleep. In the line, the only means of dealing with them was to run a burning cigarette-end down the seams of ones underclothes. I remember Smash sitting on a fire-step doing this and remarking, 'I niver saw such whoppers—the buggers has got blue eyes and clogs on.'

After I had fallen ill, the colonel came to see me, shivering on my wire-netting bed, to say that he was sending me on leave the next day.

With the fever still on me I travelled to Boulogne and across the Channel. I had a civilized meal in a restaurant, which I felt too ill to enjoy, and slept deeply on the train north. I was received with joy by my family at Newcastle Central Station but alarmed them by falling asleep again in the tram-car on the way home. I was sent to bed immediately and made to hand all my clothes to my mother so that they could be disinfected outside in the yard.

Next morning, I could hardly raise my head, but fortunately my brother, Alex, had arrived on leave, wearing captain's rank having been commissioned in the RAMC. He is a professor of zoology and an entomologist, and so he had been posted from his field ambulance to do research on louse-born diseases. His subsequent findings and writings are now medical classics. He dosed me with quinine and other drugs, and in a couple of days I was on my feet, a bit wobbly but fit to go out. Though people were very kind, like most other returned soldiers I felt out of place. We from the trenches lived in a world of our own, so different from life at home that it was difficult to communicate properly. I remember a neighbour who had invited me to a party remarking to me next day, 'Whatever did your mother say about you reaching home after midnight?' I, who only a few days before had been crawling about No Man's Land from dusk till dawn!!

Mother was very concerned to know what happened on Sundays at the front, and after I grasped what she meant, she was even more concerned to learn that hostilities continued throughout the Sabbath. To our surprise and delight, my brother Jim also turned up, having just participated in the Cambrai offensive with his unit, the 2nd Durham Light Infantry. During his leave the Germans counter-attacked at Cambrai and when we read the newspaper reports together, Jim sadly commented that the Boche was now back on his battalion's original line.

He was lucky to be out of it; and so was I, for during my absence my battalion suffered dreadfully in the Ypres salient, and two of my company officers were killed.

I was ready, even eager, to return to my unit when my leave was up, but had I known what was in store for me in a few weeks, I would not have been so keen.

Chapter 6

CANNONADE AND CATASTROPHE

LIFE in an infantry unit on the Western Front was one of hardship, discomfort and boredom punctuated with intense fear and excitement. The working men who made up the bulk of the rank and file were accustomed to some hardship in their daily lives before enlisting. They did not expect comfort in the army and certainly did not get it. In the line all ranks lived like animals in dens—dark dank dug-outs— or in clarty ditches. The expressive word clarty means muddy in Tyneside dialect and the soldiers often exclaimed 'We're up to the —— oxters in —— clarts' meaning up to the armpits in mud. I cannot remember a dry trench, even in summer, and in one platoon area we occupied we waded through a dense seething mass of live frogs. Out of the line we lived in squalid huts and tents in fug and squalor. I recall one 'rest' period we spent in bell tents in the winter of 1917, when we dared not take off our boots, for if we did they froze hard. Occasionally, officers slept on bunks made of wire-netting stretched over a wooden frame, which raised the sleepers a few inches off the floor or ground, but the rank and file rarely had even this little consolation. Looking back to those times I still marvel at the men's stoical endurance for months and years in such conditions, their acceptance of discipline and danger, not knowing when they would be free to return to their homes. Yet I cannot recall any speaking of peace without victory, or that I had to place any soldier of our company on a serious official charge.

As Uncle Toby said, speaking of the troops in Flanders

in the eighteenth century, 'they swore terribly', and they
groused continually, but this seldom led to any dereliction
of duty. If the grousing led to surliness, a wise officer or
NCO could spot the reason and remove the cause, which
was often trivial, perhaps something to do with food or
unequal allocations of tasks, and rarely about hazards in
action. My brother, Jim, reminiscing about those days
once remarked, 'Really, the only bright spots in the men's
lives were the receipt of mail and the daily tot of rum.'

When not under fire, the troops were often surprisingly
cheerful and sang Rabelasian, sentimental or fatalistic songs,
but never patriotic ditties such as the Germans did. The
first were bawdy ballads, some of them very old with
sentiments similar to those sung by Ancient Pistol and
his cronies, such as:

> 'I'd rather live at home amongst the pubs to roam
> And live on the earnings of a high class whore.'

They were bawdy enough, but the lyrics were not lewd or
sick, and I find that they were less objectionable than some
sung in the present permissive society. The sentimental
tunes were sung with deep feeling and would be laughed at
today. The numerous fatalistic songs, expressing the soldiers
reluctance to military life, may have deceived the enemy
generals when cogitating on our morale. One very popular
ditty was sung to the tune of 'What a friend we have in
Jesus', with these words:

> 'When this bloody war is over, oh! how happy I will be;
> When I get my civvy clothes on, no more soldiering for
> me;
> No more asking for a furlough, no more asking for a pass;
> You can tell the sergeant major, he can stick it up his
> arse.'

Another doleful ditty was:

> 'We started off fifty odd non coms and men
> We started off fifty and now we are ten,
> And if this bloody war doesn't end very soon
> There'll be nobody left in the ruddy platoon.'

We went in and out of the trenches for tours of days or weeks, came back into close support positions, and, very occasionally, marched back to billets in villages untouched by shell-fire. Here we did some desultory training and, after we had scraped the mud off ourselves, we were inspected by generals. A few verses published in *Punch* during the war are very descriptive but have rarely been quoted (see appendix). They are entitled 'On the road to Oonoeswhere', and they sum up the feelings of the rank and file who were given little or no information and blindly obeyed orders.

I cannot detail all the movements of our battalion, but I recall that we went in and out of the front line on various sectors from south of Peronne to north of Arras. I was lucky to miss one action in which the battalion suffered severely, as with most of my company I contracted impetigo and was sent down to the base at Rouen for a few days, and thence to a sniping and scouting course. I also was detailed to attend a lecture by a Colonel Cambell, VC, on bayonet fighting, in which he described this form of combat in such bloodthirsty language that instead of being stimulated, his audience was deterred from engaging in it. One or two incidents during my service in France are so vivid that I remember them in detail.

I had the most enjoyable meal in my life in a French farmhouse one time when I was detailed to take the company for baths in an improvised bath house and cleansing station. I asked a mam'selle if it was possible to have something to eat, as I had missed breakfast. She smiled and called out, '*Maman,*' and an old crone came to the door. '*Regardez, Maman*', said Mam'selle, '*voici ce pauvre petit officier de l'Ecosse — qu'il a faim, le jeune garçon.*'

Maman nodded and replied, '*C'est vrai. Un garçon souffre toujours de la faim; vite, la soupe et une omelette.*'

They sat me down at a rough plank table and put a bowl of steaming broth in front of me, which I drank eagerly, while Mam'selle broke four eggs into a basin. Maman brought a bottle of raw red wine and a glass and cut a fresh loaf of bread. The omelette was cooked with the centre still liquid and was delicious — the whole meal so different to our usual fare that it is still a high spot in my memories. The good women looked on, nodding kindly saying, '*C'est bon, monsieur — n'est ce pas?*'

I stammered my thanks in schoolboy French and pulled out my wallet to pay, but they would accept less than two francs. Thank you again, Maman and Mam'selle, over the years.

During Christmas and New Year 1917–18, we were in the front lines and had our Christmas dinner in one of the deep tunnels of the Hindenburg Line, part of which was now in our hands. Bitterly cold weather persisted for six weeks, and our tour occupied four of them. The ground was so frozen that little digging could be done, and we spent our time trying to keep warm. Apparently the Boche were doing the same, for there was little shooting apart from a few whizbangs, or light shells, morning and evening to denote their presence. We were on an old battlefield and there was much debris about, so on Boxing Day being rather bored I went out over the top of the support trench to find some souvenirs. I soon repented my action because there were numbers of corpses in field grey lying about half-buried in the frozen soil; it was some moments before I realized what they were since they looked like part of the landscape. As I turned to come back I discovered the entrance to an apparently untouched German dug-out and decided to explore it. The steps down were steep and slippery, so I cautiously descended backwards. Reaching the bottom I turned, and received the greatest shock of my life. Lying prone on a low bed was a gigantic German officer, dressed in his long grey greatcoat and with his steel helmet still on his head. He had been dead a long time but his features were still recognizable. The poor wretch had evidently been placed there with some care by his subordinates just before he died, and the battle had not disturbed him. I stood horror-struck for a few seconds, then fled up the steps and back to our trench, where my company commander gave me a dressing-down and called me amongst other things, a bloody fool, which indeed I was.

We simple battalion officers rarely saw or met generals other than our brigadier, so I recall two occasions on which I did.

Walking along a road one rainy day not far from Arras, a brother subaltern and I passed a slight figure in a mackintosh and an unrecognizable head-dress. Thinking him to be some local inhabitant, we took little notice of him until, when we had gone a few yards, a high peppery voice, rather like that of Field-Marshal Montgomery, shouted, 'Come here, you two young officers.'

We retraced our steps and, as he looked so fierce, thought we had better stand to attention. 'What,' he snapped, 'should you do if you meet a brother officer?'

We stood dumb, and he continued, 'You should say "Good day" and behave like gentlemen. Do you know who I am?'

We regretted that we did not. 'I am your divisional commander, General Nicholson. You do not recognize me?'

Divisional generals were far beyond our ken, but we hastily saluted and apologized. He softened a little and remarked, 'Now, you young officers must always remember that gentlemen always say "Good day" to each other whether acquainted or not. Now be off with you.'

We saluted again and hurried away feeling very temporary officers and gentlemen.

The same general did visit us in the line some time later, arriving at our company HQ dug-out having crawled the last twenty yards, since the trench had been blown in. We were a little shy, we were unaccustomed to receiving such VIPs in our home, and we felt inferior and scruffy. His first words relieved the tension, 'By Gad, you chaps, I thought a sniper would get me crawling those last few yards as my bottom's too big and sticks out a bit!'

When he had sipped a mug of tea, laced with a tot of rum, and chatted amiably, we began to think him a grand chap, although he did not tell us how we were to win the war, and when he had departed we agreed that it was damn decent for an elderly grey-haired man to crawl through all that mud to pay us a call.

Late in March 1918 our battalion was in billets behind Arras, having just completed three weeks in the front line, and we were expecting at least ten days' rest. But after four days, we were hurriedly paraded to be inspected by an officer so senior that few had ever heard of him, although he turned out to be our army commander, General Rawlinson. We stood in the mud on a drizzling morning, a bedraggled body of troops muffled in drab, muddy greatcoats near the ancient field of Agincourt, trying to look soldierly. We did not succeed, for by this time in the war the quality of reinforcements was extremely poor, many of them of low medical categories, and we were sadly under strength. My platoon numbered twenty-two all ranks, and in one of my sections the lance corporal was the only fit man — of the three privates one was deaf, one almost blind and one mentally sub-normal.

When the great man appeared on horseback with his aide and with two outriders holding pennants, the battalion pulled itself up to attention with a loud squelch. 'Stand your men at ease,' commanded the general to our colonel. 'I wish to address them but have no time to inspect the ranks.'

Though we were not keen on inspections, we felt aggrieved that he was not going to look at us after our efforts to clean ourselves up.

Still sitting on his horse, the great man continued, 'I regret that I must cut short your period of rest and return you to the front line tomorrow. As you know by intelligence reports, the Russians have made a separate peace with Germany which has freed many German divisions for action on the Western Front. They are under command of the famous victorious General Ludendorff who has placed them opposite our positions, which are not fully manned as we have had to take over some miles from the French army. We shall be greatly outnumbered and outgunned. Ludendorff will use many tanks and probably a new gas of a most penetrating type. The supporting trenches which you have been digging are not yet complete but our orders are to hold on to every inch of ground. It is doubtful if I shall be able to visit you in the trenches but I shall be waiting to welcome you when you return having repulsed the greatest military onslaught in history. Good luck to you all.'

He turned his horse and rode away over the field of Agincourt leaving a stunned silence, until one of the men in the front rank of my platoon spoke up in a loud voice, 'That general felly missed a bit oot. He nivor telt us it's gannin to rain as weel.'

On the evening of 19th March, we marched up to the front over rough tracks. As usual, when we were due for a battle, our pipers played us up, and so two rather inexpert pipers marched in front of my company blowing their pipes almost without ceasing for five miles, directly into the ears of my men. When we arrived at the entrance to the communication trench, they stood aside and saluted, and one remarked, 'Good-bye, sor, good luck, lads. I hope it is not gannin to be too bad for ye.'

One of my platoon, I believe it was Smash, replied briskly, 'Ye bugger, if it's any worse than ye've put us through in the last five miles it'll be bloody morder.'

I can still see the look on the breathless piper's face!

My company was in reserve to the battalion and was located in a narrow railway cutting labelled Bunhill Row; our firing positions were in a trench twenty yards forward of it. The map showed that at one time a narrow gauge railway had connected Croisilles, on our left, to Ecoust and Bullecourt, on our right. We had barely settled into some sketchy dug-outs when the colonel sent for me and ordered me to take the platoon over the top that night, 20th March, and to enter the German lines to take a prisoner.

We were all weary having carried loads up to the line, but at 20.00 hours we set off towards the front line trench, lightly equipped, with our faces blacked, carrying rifles, clubs and grenades. I reported to the company commander in the front line, who said that all was suspiciously quiet; his men would give us covering fire if necessary and would try not to shoot us on the way back. It was a dark murky night, suitable for this nefarious type of work; we crawled in and out of shell-holes until we came to the German wire, which we found in poor repair and about twenty yards deep. There were some gaps, and picking our way through we came to the enemy firing trench. It was a proper trench, not an abandoned field-work, and had a typical German smell so different from our own. Leaving a sentry, we dropped into it and made our way cautiously along it for about fifty yards. All was deathly quiet and spooky, but there were plenty of recent traces of Boche — bits of equipment, water bottles and stick grenades, but no bodies, alive or dead. Expecting to be challenged at any moment, we stole around traverses with our hearts in our mouths, clutching our grenades. Eventually, we came to a latrine where the enemy had been using old shrapnel helmets as chamber pots, and not long before. There were lots of odd papers about and, to the indignation of the men, I ordered them to be collected, and for two chamber pots to be carried away for possible intelligence and proof that we had been where we said. We went a few yards down a communication trench and found nothing, so as time was getting on we made our way back over No Man's Land as cautiously as we had come. The front line OC gave us badly needed mugs of tea and rum, and we trudged back down Pelican Avenue on the right flank of the battalion area. The colonel was again disappointed that we had not obtained a prisoner, but he believed my report when I showed him the evidence and dismissed me to my company, which I reached at about 04.15 on 21st March.

I was relating our experiences to my captain when there came a sudden flash which lit up the whole sky, then a tremendous crash, as thousands of German shells landed at the same moment on the British lines. To quote Churchill's words, 'The greatest cannonade in history had begun.'

We ducked for cover, and my OC shouted, 'You damned little liar, you said there were no Germans over there.'

It was some years before my story was proved true, when the official histories stated that the enemy had vacated their lines and withdrawn several hundred yards before they advanced to the assault.

The shelling was the worst anyone had experienced, even

on the Somme, and as we flattened ourselves against the forward walls of the dug-outs, we could communicate only by signs, for most of the time we could not hear ourselves speak. Fortunately, most of the projectiles hit the far bank of the cutting, and at first we escaped with few casualties. During a brief slackening of the bombardment, we were ordered to man the fire trench in front. When we gained it we discovered that it was only two feet deep, so we all knelt down and started digging frantically with our entrenching tools constantly bespattered by earth thrown up by the explosions. Though it was now dawn we could see barely three yards around us because the countryside was enveloped in thick fog. In one way, this was an advantage, since the German gunners could not fire by direct observation—a few yards' correction of aim would have killed the lot of us. Additionally, the fog damped down the noise of the projectiles coming at us, and we could only feel the explosions. Oddly enough, we could distinctly hear the rat-tat-tat of our heavy machine-guns which fired from rising ground behind the cutting until they were knocked out. The storm of shells lasted for nearly two hours. Then our bodies began quivering, we were all gasping for breath, and beginning to feel drowsy when we heard a gas alarm, followed by some duller explosions. We clawed on our masks, revolted by their smell, and within moments the eye-pieces clouded up so that we were partially blinded. One or two men who had not put their masks on properly were led away coughing.

I heard a runner call my name, and I was told to report to battalion HQ. I groped my way back into Bunhill Row, where I found my captain with his mask off his face but with the mouth- and nose-piece *in situ*. I removed mine and found that the gas was less dense and that it did not affect the eyes. Just then a stretcher party carrying a casualty came down the cutting, when a shell landed practically on top of it, killing all instantly, except one bearer, who was dreadfully wounded in the throat. The poor man, spouting blood, crawled on his stomach towards the company HQ dug-out, and I pray I may never again in my life see such an appalling sight. We tried to restrain him so that we could stop the bleeding, but he could not understand and tried to writhe away from us. As we held him down he became still, and my captain shook his head sadly, 'No need for dressings now; he's finished.'

Taking the soldier's pocket book from his tunic he looked at it and exclaimed, 'Good God, the poor lad was only eighteen, bloody scandalous to send him out here.'

The barrage now seemed to be lifting, so I ran down to battalion HQ and reported to the colonel. 'Peacock,' he ordered, 'you will take two platoons and form a flank down Pelican Avenue to the right of our area and try to join up with our forward companies.'

He showed me a trench map and said that in his opinion the Germans had broken through the unit of the 59th Division on our right; it was possible that our forward companies were intact, although no reports from them had come through for some time.

When I emerged from the HQ the enemy shells were bursting fifty yards or more behind us, indicating that the Germans had advanced and did not wish to be caught in their own barrage. So my own and one other platoon were able to make our way up Pelican Avenue; we posted sections every twenty-five yards to start building fire-steps, since the trench was very deep. As we worked the fog lifted a little, and we saw hundreds of men about four hundred yards away towards Bullecourt, some moving forward and some back. At first, we were inclined to cheer, thinking that the Germans had been repulsed; but when we looked through binoculars we saw that those moving towards the west were British prisoners. I happened to look back towards the railway cutting and was astounded to see figures in field-grey on the rising ground behind it. The Germans were gradually enveloping our battalion area, and the first German soldiers whom I saw distinctly on that dismal day were behind us!

We were now joined by some stragglers from the 59th Division, and soon men of our forward company staggered down the trench, all glassy-eyed and dazed; their company commander was with them and had, I think, been blown up by a shell and was almost incoherent. I asked what was happening, and he muttered something about moving to the left flank along the support trench called Tiger, which ran between the front and Bunhill Row, and suggested my platoons form a rearguard. He stumbled on, and that was the last I ever saw of him. Within a few minutes they were followed by Germans hurling stick bombs in front of them, and we saw others advancing from the direction of Bullecourt. Sergeant Soulsby fired off a Lewis gun in this direction, but it soon jammed. We panicked a little and were driven back into Tiger trench; this was very deep and had no fire-steps, so we could not see over the top. We blocked it by hacking down the sides and mounted another Lewis gun, but the Germans ran along in the open and showered us with grenades, causing more panic. One of these fell behind me, and I felt a blow on the lower spine. Later, I discovered that my belt buckle had protected me from a serious wound, but a small piece of metal had entered my back and I still retain it. Soulsby fired off a magazine and then, when the enemy were almost on top of him, he dismantled the gun and threw the pieces away so that they could not use it. He was captured there. Those of us still on our feet fled back along the trench and emerged on open ground, where, for the first and last time in my service, we fanned out into open order, lay down in the prone position and began rapid rifle fire. There were only eight of us left of the two platoons, and we fired a great number of rounds. These delayed the enemy for a short time, until a German officer in a red-lined cloak and coloured hat signalled up a machine-gun, which sprayed us with bullets; we retired on our stomachs to a ditch where we found an officer trying to organize some defence. This was soon disorganized by low-flying aircraft firing machine-guns, enfilading us. I could assemble only five men now and thought it my duty to report back to Battalion HQ, a foolish decision as it turned out, for the enemy had nearly surrounded it. I put myself into the bag just before the Boche closed the opening, while the other officer escaped.

I found the HQs of two battalions in a deep dug-out, with

the two colonels sitting hopefully by a telephone. They were not particularly interested in my report, probably knowing more about the general situation than I did, and were waiting for a counter-attack by another brigade, which never came. Returning to the top of the dug-out, I found the cutting full of officers and men, and several Lewis guns out of action and covered in mud. Except to the rear, there was no field of view. It was sudden death to look over the top. Our intelligence officer, did so; he was immediately shot through the forehead and rolled down dead at our feet.

One fatal casualty horrified me more than others, for lying in the cutting was the body of a middle-aged man who, I think, at one time had been a sergeant in another unit and had then been reduced in rank. On the sleeve of his tunic were four wound stripes, which indicated that he had been returned time and time again to the fighting, but that he should have been withdrawn from it entirely. I doubt if any veteran such as he would have been so misused in the Second World War, when there was a great difference in attitude of high command.

We were in a desperate plight and in an untenable position, though now with hindsight, I think many of us could have got away by an organized break-out to the left flank (Colonel Acklom and his adjutant tried this but were killed). We had been trained for static war, to hold on to a few yards of ground or ditch, and no one suggested any other tactics. More than half a century later, I can still remember some of my reactions at the time, and I feel sure they were very similar to those of others present. I was very frightened and anxious, with a leaden weight in my stomach; but fortunately I was not terrified, as terror is not the same as fear and induces crazy actions which are often fatal. I was so dreadfully tired from lack of sleep and food and from physical effort and the effects of the bombardment that my senses were dulled and I had ceased to care what happened.

Through the smoke and gloom we suddenly saw a line of figures in field grey, some assisting others, crossing our rear; we opened fire before we realized that they were wounded making their way to Ecoust, oblivious that a pocket of British were still holding on. We ceased fire and let them pass.

We did hold on for a time by throwing grenades over the top of the cutting. I was told later that the Germans had been shouting at us to surrender or they would blast us with mortar shells, but I have no recollection of this, being by now practically an automaton. I had just thrown a grenade and had turned to pick up another from the box; when I straightened up, I saw a dozen Germans a few feet away in the cutting. I was so appalled that I stood paralysed, until a black-bearded *feldwebel* pointed a Luger pistol at my stomach and remarked threateningly, '*Sie werfen Granaten*' (You throw grenades). Fortunately, I had not drawn the pin of the grenade that I was holding, so I dropped it. Then, to my everlasting gratitude, a German officer, who may have been the one we had been trying to shoot, pushed away the NCO's pistol and told me to take off my belt. Other officers and men were as dumbfounded as I and probably were receiving the same treatment, but no one actually raised their hands in surrender. I do distinctly remember a colonel coming up from a dug-out and exclaiming, 'Shall we surrender or die like English gentlemen?', and the thought flashing through my brain, 'If he decides to fight, I shall be one of the first dead!'

Numbers of men came up from other dug-outs, and the colonel, almost in tears, said, 'Good God, I did not know we had these left to fight with.'

In the end, we were marshalled into a column and escorted back through the enemy lines. I recall little of the march, being asleep on my feet most of the time. We eventually came to a road along which thousands of enemy reinforcements were marching, and then to an enormous barbed wire enclosure. There, though it was raining hard, I lay on the ground and slept the sound sleep of a youngster; I was still a teenager.

Chapter 7

IN AND OUT OF PRISON

I AWOKE after several hours, refreshed but abominably hungry. The compound was now crowded with British prisoners, and a column of them was just arriving. A brisk bespectacled German officer greeted them with a pleasant, 'Good morning, gentlemen, all 34th Division, I suppose?' Before wiser men could stop them, several shouted, 'I'm 59th', '3rd', etc. The German smiled again and thanked them for the information. (Military prisoners are only supposed to give name, rank and number.) Later that day I met a young subaltern who had been captured earlier and alone. He told me he had been courteously grilled and when asked the units of his brigade, had invented some peculiar ones and gave incorrect answers to other questions. He was dismissed courteously, but on presenting himself to receive some food the intelligence officer shook his head, saying, 'No breakfast for you today, Lieutenant; you tell colossal lies.'

More or less the same thing happened to an RFC pilot who said his plane was powered by a 'Freeman, Hardy and Willis' engine.

At mid-morning some buckets of fish soup, which smelled foul and tasted worse, were brought to us. Many prisoners had no eating utensils, having been stripped of their equipment, and none were provided. Another officer and I tossed up for whose tin hat should be used as a soup bowl. I lost, stripped the lining from my hat and received a ration of the hell-broth. I have never tasted anything so foul before or since and though we were ravenous, most of us could tolerate only a spoonful, but we ate a little black bread with relish. Few of us had taken any food for over thirty-six hours, since what we had with us in Bunhill Row was fouled by gas and dangerous. We were pleased to eat anything, and we happily drank ersatz coffee made from acorns.

We were marched back through French countryside untouched by shell-fire and through poverty-stricken villages in which the poor French peasants, seeing our hunger, threw us turnips and carrots. I caught a carrot and marched along chewing it like a rabbit. The roads were packed with enemy transport, much of it civilian vehicles drawn by scrawny horses. There were open carriages, growlers and hansom cabs as well as farm carts. A veteran of the South African War, walking by my side, said, 'Cheer up, Pip. We'll be home by Christmas. If this is all the transport they have, the Boche will never reach the Channel ports and this is their last fling.'

He was a good prophet.

We were interned for a few days in a warehouse in Cambrai. Here a few pails of water were provided for several hundred prisoners to wash with, and after one or two had washed, the rest of us decided to remain dirty.

About ten days after the battle, we were entrained for the long trip to Germany. I was lucky to get into the only proper coach, the rest being cattle trucks, and I spent about four days on a luggage rack. At long intervals, we were given bowls of soup and a slice of bread, and we began to feel real starvation. After a fair amount of experience as a prisoner, I find that one of the greatest trials is diarrhoea, especially on long, confined journeys, where eventually the captives find themselves travelling in a mobile latrine.

Our destination was Rastatt in South Germany where a hutted camp had been built; it was reasonably comfortable, but food so scarce that soon we were ravenous and emaciated. Even as a prisoner of the Japanese years later, I was never so hungry as in that camp, still having a boy's appetite. To be fair, the Germans could hardly provide better fare, as due to our blockade they were almost starving themselves. Lack of food soon leads to lack of consideration for others

77

and turns men into something akin to beasts. I remember in this camp two full colonels squabbling over a few potato peelings which they had found in a dustbin; and throwing myself on a piece of stale black bread which a Cossack prisoner had thrown over the wire to me, and growling like a dog as I gnawed at it.

After a few weeks in Rastatt, we were divided into parties and despatched by train to permanent camps. I was sent to a newly-established one in Phorzheim not far from Karlsruhe and Rastatt. It was a small, three-storied elementary school built on the banks of the River Enz in a suburb of the town. The school playground was our parade ground and exercise yard. We could not complain about our accommodation as there were toilets and flush WCs, and sixteen officers slept in each classroom on wooden bunks with straw mattresses with a blanket and a sheet. The food was better cooked than at Rastatt, in a kitchen supervised by a German frau of immense proportions, but it was still meagre in quantity. Every three days each prisoner received a roll of bread six inches long, which we tried unsuccessfully to refrain from eating all at once, and once a week we got a small piece of roasted horse-flesh sausage. The basic diet was sauerkraut, which smelt and tasted revolting, and a few potatoes. However, after a couple of months, Red Cross parcels arrived; the guards who opened them were staggered at the sight of food they had not seen for years. With this food, we started to put on weight again; we felt stronger and began to talk of escape, which would have been difficult since no one knew much geography and since there were no maps available as in older-established camps. We had been stripped to the skin on entering the school and thoroughly searched, and anything which might have aided escape had been removed. A friend of mine did retain a compass by the very simple subterfuge of holding it loosely in his half-clenched hand during the examination.

Our captors had posted a war map on the wall of a room we called our library, with little flags to indicate the positions of the opposing forces. At first, those representing German troops had progressed steadily towards the Channel ports, to the great delight of the guards, who actually provided us with local newspapers so that we could check the facts. The flags remained fairly static during the summer, but as autumn came they began to move back to the French frontier, slowly at first and then in bounds as the Allies advanced. The German officers looked grave. We rejoiced, and roll calls became so rowdy that the senior British officer, a staff colonel who was captured while rallying stragglers in the March battle, had to check us so that parade could be over in reasonable time. At roll calls, a German adjutant with an interpreter counted us in files; he then read out the name of each prisoner who then stepped out of the ranks, saluted and marched off. As each officer did so, the interpreter would remark to his superior, '*Jawohl*' meaning, 'that is the person named.' We adopted the practice of repeating it, but using a lewd, similar-sounding English expression! I am sure the interpreter understood this, but he joined in the joke as the German officer gravely bowed and returned each salute.

Soon after our arrival in this camp, we were asked to sign a *parole card* — I have mine still — which stated something to this effect: 'I, Lt. Peacock, undertake not to escape or make any preparations to do so while out of camp for exercise in official parties.' Having signed this, we were allowed to join a party conducted by unarmed sentries to take a short walk in the neighbouring countryside. At first we were too weak to take exercise, but towards the end, we were stronger and asked for permission to play football! A field was found and a small deduction made from our funds (we received a little POW money) for rent.

As a rugby football had been sent to us by the Red Cross, I again had the opportunity of playing scrum-half when we arranged sides. Our German commandant, an enormous man looking very like Hindenburg, who constantly wore his *pickelhaube* head-dress and sword, came to see our first match. He arrived, accompanied by his adjutant and an interpreter, just after the game had begun. Instead of behaving like a sensible spectator, he walked straight on to the pitch, expecting everyone to halt and stand to attention. A line of our forwards swept down the field and he became involved in a loose scrum, in which he lost both his helmet and his dignity. I had been thrown to the ground, and I found myself at his feet looking at his field-boots. The interpreter, chuckling a little at his colonel's discomforture, blew a whistle, and we all stood to attention. Assuming his *pickelhaube*, which someone had retrieved for him, he sent for our senior officer and stormed at him in a loud voice, 'You English have no manners. You call yourselves officers, but you are not gentlemen as in the German Army.'

Our senior officer replied hotly, 'It is you, Herr Colonel, who have no manners. No English gentleman would dream of interrupting a game of football without first consulting the referee.'

Such are the differences in outlook which make communications between races so difficult.

During October 1918, we noticed a definite deterioration in German discipline. The guards were mainly elderly burghers, there were only a few younger men who had had service at the front, and up to then they had marched about rather like toy soldiers. Now they slouched about on their sentry posts, smoking long pipes and cigars and becoming quite chatty with the prisoners. Some brought us newspapers and announced '*Krieg bald kaputt*' (War soon finish. (We replied '*Ja, ja, das ist gut.*'

Then, early in November our senior officer, to his astonishment, was approached by a German lance-corporal who, standing strictly to attention, announced that there had been a sort of revolution and as President of the Local Soldiers and Sailors Council, he was now in charge of the camp, and that the officers had been dismissed. He was not greeted with any enthusiasm by our colonel, who told him sharply that he expected the administration to be conducted according to International Law.

Then came the news of the Armistice, which the Germans called '*Waffenstillstand*'. There was little cheering as the word went round, for we had nothing to celebrate with because with the confusion in Germany at the time our parcels had stopped. Some of us expected immediate freedom, and we were astounded when our English adjutant posted an order which read something like this:

'I hereby notify all ranks in this camp that they are now in a unit of the British Army and as senior officer, I assume command. Strict discipline will be maintained and my orders obeyed. Any officer or other rank attempting to leave this camp and make his way to the British Lines will be court-martialled on return to UK.

Signed

. . . . Colonel'

There was a good deal of grousing, but no one dared to tackle the colonel, who was a stern, distant, regular officer. He was becoming increasingly irritated by the German lance-corporal, who repeatedly consulted him about what he should do now that he was in high office. After a few days, the colonel brusquely ordered him to bring back his own officers, as the administration was getting into a mess. They came back but, at the insistence of their men, without their epaulettes, badges of rank or swords, and looking so downcast that we were almost sorry for them. They explained that the situation in the town was so uncertain that guards had to be retained not to keep us confined, but to protect us from mutineers and hot-heads seeking revenge.

Newspapers were still delivered to the camp, and I still have a few pages of one which has a large cartoon depicting 'Hans', a farmer, reaping his harvest, with the caption 'And the Fatherland remains untouched'. I have often recalled this caption and wondered whether there would have been a Second World War if the Allies had firmly occupied the country east of the Rhine.

Within a very short time Phorzheim and the surrounding district quietened down. Officers were permitted to visit the town and were even able to obtain some German currency by writing cheques on British banks. When a friend and I walked down to the main square on a Sunday morning, everything was peaceable, the burghers strolling about in their Sunday best. There were one or two armed police about, and these were guarding food shops, which had notices plastered on their windows saying, '*Wer plundert wird evschossen*' (Plunderers will be shot). We entered a large café and sat down on a banquette. No one took much notice of us, but we felt embarrassed in our tattered uniform. There were some large cakes, apparently thick with cream, on a counter, so we ordered two slices to eat with our ersatz coffee. Both were a disappointment, as the cream on the cake was also ersatz and consisted of beer froth sweetened with saccharine. Only one person besides the waiter spoke to us, a fat prosperous-looking type who remarked to me, 'Shift your bottom up a bit, Lieutenant, so I can get mine on the seat.'

He had spent many years in London and was hoping to return there as soon as possible.

Then there was the sound of martial music approaching, and we rushed out to see what was happening. The main *strasse* was '*mit Fahnen bedeckt*' and crowded with spectators; along came a large regiment of German troops, in full marching order, headed by a military band of fifty or more musicians playing the popular marching tune '*Püppchen du bist mein Augenstern*' as only a German band can. These troops were not a beaten rabble; headed by their officers mounted on chargers, they marched well with their heads up, and looked tough disciplined fighting soldiers. Some women rushed forward to give them slices of black bread and jam, and girls threw flowers. Fascinated as always to see soldiers, I took up a position near a lamp-post to watch them go by, and had a good view of their regimental commander riding behind the band on a fine black horse. He was youngish, in a smart tight-waisted uniform, wearing a monocle on his duel-scarred face, and he looked devilishly efficient. He caught sight of me and raised his hand in salute, and I was so impressed that I came to attention and returned the salute. Then a drunken soldier in the crowd gave me a shoulder charge and I almost fell over. Since then I have often wondered if Ludendorff's claim that his army was not beaten didn't have some truth in it. I feel sure that twenty years later that regimental commander, promoted to the rank of general and mounted on a tank, led a *blitzkrieg* somewhere, and I am glad that I was not in front of him when he did so.

Oddly enough, my friend and I decided to attend church, so we entered a Lutheran one and stole up into the gallery. There was a full congregation; I remember one of the hymns, '*Eine feste Burg ist unser Gott*', and snatches of the sermon, which exhorted the *volk* to lift up their hearts and to work to restore the Fatherland. Most of the worshippers in the gallery were young *backfische* (flappers) who paid more attention to us than to the pastor; as we were leaving, a pert one brushed up against me not altogether accidentally, and I apologized in German. She giggled, and remarked to a friend, 'So these English officers appear quite approachable.' An older lady spoke sharply to them, and they fled.

On our way back to camp we were also given what used to be termed 'the glad eye', and we stopped to talk with two frauleins. An elderly corporal of the camp guard coming by barked something at them, and they hurried away, then he turned to us and said in broken English, 'Herren Offiziere, you are young men and I am old enough to be your father. Take the advice of a corporal and do not speak to such *Fraulein* as they are wicked and *nix gut* will come to you. The *Krieg ist jetzt beendet* and you must *wiederrgehen* to your *Vater und Mutter*.'

He was a decent old boy and quite right; we learned later that these girls had had their hair cropped short to indicate that they had been intimate with the enemy.

There were several false alarms regarding repatriation, and on one occasion we threw nearly all our Red Cross biscuits to crowds of hungry children who were standing outside the school. They crammed them into their mouths, and we realized that they were more than hungry, they were starving—all except one, about six years old, well dressed and in charge of a nanny, who spurned any biscuit that fell near him and who put out his tongue and spat in our direction. I feel sure that he joined the SS later in life. I gave a tin of cocoa and a few biscuits to an old photographer who had taken pictures of us for the parole cards; I was embarrassed by his gratitude, when he remarked, 'Ach Herr Leutnant, you will save the life of my daughter who is dying from lack of real food.'

He sent me Christmas cards for several years afterwards asking me to visit his family at any time.

At last we had orders to move, and we marched in column of route to the railway station, where to our astonishment a train of first-class carriages was waiting. As officers, even enemies still had some standing in the Reich! A young German lieutenant conducted us, now wearing his sword again. He had been badly wounded and was more affable to us than the other Germans in the camp, declaring that he hoped it would be all over before he had to return to the front. He had always been civil, and after the Armistice he asked me jokingly, 'Is it true that you were to make an attempt to escape in the commandant's clothes?'

The commandant was nearly seven feet tall and about six feet round. This officer also commented that we would not have been successful escaping via the roof, a project we had discussed. As the train pulled out, he saluted several times gravely and courteously, and I am glad to remember that we gave him a cheer.

We exchanged trains at the Swiss frontier and were much less comfortable; then we halted for a night at Pontalier, the frontier station in France, where the population turned out to cheer us, and many accompanied us to our billet. We were allowed out, and I was grabbed by a charming madamoiselle who was waiting at the barrack gate like a First World War Lili Marlene; she took me off to her home, where I was introduced to Papa and Maman and two brave Poilus, still wearing bright blue coats and zouave trousers. My schoolboy French was our only means of communication, but we got on together famously, and shared a typical French meal of soup, crusty bread, meat and red wine, the best food I had eaten since my capture. I was uncertain of my way back to barracks, and so it was suggested that Mademoiselle should conduct me; this was an exciting idea, as she was most comely and just my age. We walked through the darkening town babbling in two languages, and romance was blooming, but to our dismay

Papa had put on his boots and followed us at ten paces behind, which he continued to do until we reached the barracks, where we solemnly shook hands as I said, '*Merci.*'

But she managed to whisper, '*Je reviens le matin.*'

She kept her promise in time for us to exchange a few simple but fervent kisses behind the guardroom before we moved off to our train. It consisted now of cattle trucks, and we made a slow and hungry journey across France to Boulogne. There I recall Lena Aswell's concert, a forerunner of ENSA, and Leslie Henson, who made us laugh a bit.

Across the Channel, we assembled again at Folkestone, where we were each handed a letter from His Majesty the King welcoming us home; and then we were documented and sent on leave.

I detrained once more at Newcastle Central, to be returned to the bosom of my family in time for Christmas, and for the second time saw my mother wave a Union Jack to hail a soldier home. She said, with rare tears in her eyes, 'Thinking of you starving and hungry, I choked over my food for the last nine months.' Although she was usually undemonstrative, I knew that she had a deep love for her children. My father, a very sensitive man, after greeting me warmly resorted to poetry: 'His helmet now shall make a hive for bees.'

But this was not yet to be.

During my period of leave, I received a letter from the War Office, similar to that sent to all officer prisoners, directing me to submit a report of the circumstances of my capture. I did so in some detail, describing the engagement of 21st March, 1918, which may have added a few facts to official histories of the German offensive. A few weeks later, I received an official notice from the adjutant general's branch informing me that a committee had considered it and were pleased to inform me that no blame could be attached to me for becoming a prisoner of war.

I could have claimed immediate demobilization, but I was reluctant to do so since I had no money except my soldier's pay. I was attracted to no other profession than soldiering, or, as second best, the colonial police; so when I reported to my depot at East Boldon again and discovered that they wanted volunteers for the Rhine Army of Occupation, I put my name down. My parents were surprised and disappointed, having thought that I would now be thankful to stay in a safe and comfortable home. I never mentioned to them that our battalion transport officer, who owned a large farm in South Africa, had offered to take me on as his pupil and possibly his successor, for I knew that they would have been terribly distressed if I had emigrated. Mother especially liked to have her chicks all about her in the same town. I have often wondered if I made the right decision, since no doubt life on a South African farm would have been interesting and romantic, and might possibly have led to prosperity and even riches.

A brigade of four battalions of young soldiers assembled at Catterick Camp, and there I joined the 54th Battalion Northumberland Fusiliers. The officers and some NCOs had seen active service, but none of the junior ranks had, since most of them were teenagers, lately conscripted, and not eligible for demobilization, and most were reluctant soldiers needing coddling at times. They did not enjoy the long train journey from Dunkirk to Cologne, and said so. My battalion occupied Marienberg Barracks, the very comfortable pre-war HQ of a German regiment. The officers were billeted in private houses, and I occupied a pleasant bedroom in the house of a rich wine-grower. It was no hardship for the family, as there were plenty of rooms; they lived in some state with a cook, gardener and maid, and my rations made a welcome addition to their food. My batman lived in too, and in no time was being bossed around by the *Hochfrau* — the wife — who, having little to do, with her husband frequently away from home, often asked me to take coffee and drinks with her in the drawing-room and was delighted when I brought some chocolate or sweets from the canteen. Looking back, I wonder . . . My wife declares that I was very innocent. On one occasion I arrived home very muddy after playing rugby with my men, and the *Hochfrau* was scandalized: 'Fancy,' she declared, 'covering yourself with dirt like that — and with common soldiers. No German officer would demean himself in such a fashion. Take a bath immediately and do not behave like a water rat and shake yourself on the floor.'

Our duties in Cologne were mainly guards and supervising the dismantling of arms and ammunition, which was done by the factory workers who had made them. There was an entire company on guard at the docks; these were very extensive, and the harbour master was pleased to have us as he was afraid of 'Bolshevism'. He once remarked, 'When your first squadron of cavalry trotted across Hohenzollern Bridge and turned into my docks, I said, "*Gott sei Dank*, we are now safe".'

The populace was on the point of starvation, although the rich could always obtain foods such as duck and chicken at the expensive restaurants. There was plenty to drink, and because the rate of exchange was falling persistently we officers could obtain a haversack full of Germany money in return for a five-pound cheque on an English bank. The Rhinelanders like to enjoy themselves, and they frequented cafés where they could drink and watch cabarets. The Café Simplizissimus, in the Hohestrasse, now defunct I gather, was an enormous place with seating for several hundred and a proper stage. On one occasion when I was having a quiet beer, a nubile lady singer wandering among the tables suddenly put her arms about me, exclaiming for all to hear, '*Ach, hier ist ein kleiner Bübchenoffizier der noch nicht geküsst ist*' (Ah—here is a little baby officer not yet been kissed); and she then gave me several smacking great kisses, to the amusement of several hundred *herrenvolk*.

We had a little excitement during our occupation when, just before the peace treaty was signed at Versailles, we were moved up to the frontier of unoccupied Germany to advance on Berlin if necessary. Thankfully, the Government of the Reich signed the Treaty, so that there was no need, and our untrained young soldiers never met the remains of the tough German army, which would probably have cut them to pieces.

To celebrate the peace several of us, junior officers, fired some WD rockets and flares; we were immediately charged for them by the quartermaster-general.

This really ended my first period of active service because I was soon sent on an education course and listed for early demobilization, since my commanding officer said that it was about time I thought of studying for a profession. He pointed out that there was an ample number of regular army officers, some reduced in rank to fill appointments in the post-war army, so I had no chance to make the army my profession. Although I was very dejected, I saw that he was right, and I was posted to Ripon and demobilized. When handed my papers by a very junior assistant adjutant, he detailed me to march a draft of several hundred men to the station to ensure that they did not begin celebrating their release in the pubs. Being ill-tempered because of leaving the army I objected vehemently saying that there were many newly-commissioned officers in the camp who could take this duty. The assistant adjutant immediately reported me with the result that during the last few minutes of my service before returning to civilian life I stood for the first time at attention in an orderly room and received a brisk ticking off by a commanding officer.

For the last time for some years I stepped off the train at Newcastle in uniform. Within a few days I had borrowed a civilian suit, not unlike what is considered modern and fashionable today, waisted with tight trousers. It felt cold and strange after my service dress, and my mother was delighted to see me wearing it, life immediately became dull; many of my friends had gone never to return and I was too sad for a lad of just twenty-one. My father guessing my thoughts had an apt quotation — 'Oh withered is the garland of the war, The soldiers pole is fallen; young boys and girls are level now with men, The odds is gone . . .'

Although I was yet to see more active service in the army, my memories of campaigning on the Western Front, even if they are less horrendous than those of many other ex-soldiers, are still the most vivid of all. 'Old men forget', but old men who as youngsters took part in battles of the First World War can never forget their experiences there. To quote my brother Jim 'They are cemented into the very fabric of our lives.'

THE LONG
FURLOUGH

Chapter 8

STUDENT IN CIVVY STREET

WHILE I was attending an army education course in Cologne, a kindly instructor, knowing I was keen to remain in the army, suggested that I first study medicine and that after qualification I should apply for a regular commission in the Royal Army Medical Corps. It seemed a good idea, and I presented myself at the Medical School of Durham University, in Newcastle, in September 1919, hoping to be registered as a medical student.

Scores of others had the same aim, and it seemed that a 'shower' of ex-servicemen had fallen on the building that registration day. Many were still in uniform, having been hastily demobilized to attend; they had arrived from all battle fronts, and one late arrival, who had joined the army as early as 1914 and should have been discharged very soon after the Armistice, came breathless from Dunster Force on the Caspian Sea. We sat in the hall of the college, swapping experiences, and we were delighted to hear the bursar announce that he would interview ex-service candidates first. I remember a red-headed young girl, straight from school, who was sitting near by remarking pettishly to a friend: 'Why should men just because they have been in the army go in front of lady students like us?' and I realized that 'the soldiers' pole had fallen', and that we were no longer heroes.

When my turn came to be interviewed, I discovered that I needed a matriculation certificate in Latin, which I did not have although I was studying it at the time; and so I was told to apply again in the following year. It seemed a very long time to wait as I had no money except a small war gratuity, and I would have no student's grant until I registered. As I was turning disconsolately away, a clerk told me that the Royal College of Surgeons was prepared to accept candidates for their dental diploma who did not have a qualification in Latin, and that if I made that diploma my aim, I could be accepted as a student at the dental school attached to the university. Without much thought, I jumped at the chance, making one of the most important decisions of my life; dentistry provided me with a livelihood for many years and led me to a much more exciting life than could be expected from such a mundane occupation.

Few members of the dental profession acquire much merit, honour or gratitude. Patients speak of the gentle, wise physician, the glamorous skilful surgeon, the blessed doctor, but never, except slightingly, of the blessed dentist, and this is a certain disadvantage in one's social life. In one way this is curious, as there are no amateurs in dentistry, the training is long and difficult, and a worthy practitioner must have a fair knowledge of medicine and surgery, not to mention manual dexterity.

My generation of students were chronically hard up, and at times had to sponge off friends to buy a cup of coffee. Most of us worked hard, anxious to qualify and earn a living, having lost valuable time in the services; but some of our teachers, accustomed to young students, seemed to deprecate our independence of thought and actions, but they had not been involved in the war. I remember our elderly and kindly dean addressing us at a special meeting on something he called 'Bolshivism amongst undergraduates', and no one to this day understands what he was referring to, except perhaps to our occasional bad manners. I wonder what that dear old man would have thought of a modern students' demo.

In 1921, during the time of the troubles in Ireland, there was a general strike of all colliery workers, and a possibility of sabotage in the mines. One day, while I was attending to a patient in the hospital, I was called out to the waiting-room, where I found an army major in plain clothes who asked to have a few words with me in private. He told me that a military defence force was being created to guard strategic points, and especially coal mines. He had obtained my name from Roland Wood, my friend from Junior Training League times, who had suggested that I might like to put on uniform again for a few months. Reminding me that this conversation was confidential, the major informed me that the defence force was to be based on the Territorial Army units, but that for reasons of diplomacy this reserve force was not to be mobilized.

What actually happened was that TA personnel were asked if they would join the new force for three months; since most of them accepted, new units were simply the old ones under different names. As most of the TA personnel in the North-east were miners who were on strike at the time, they found themselves guarding their own pits, receiving army pay as well as trades union strike pay; everyone was happy except the mine owners.

I was very tempted to accept, but I had an important examination within a few weeks and asked if I could do so later, and in the meantime join the Territorials. The strike and the defence force faded out, but I was commissioned as a lieutenant in the 4th Bn. The Northumberland Fusiliers. I was promoted to captain after a short time and commanded a company at Newburn-on-Tyne, where Captain Roland Wood commanded another in the same drill hall. The rank and file consisted mainly of miners and factory hands; many had been wartime soldiers and some pre-war Territorials.

My company sergeant major was one of many delightful characters in the battalion. His name was Luke Stewart, his age was uncertain and certainly bore no affinity to that on his military documents. He had fought in the Sudan, the Boer War, and the Great War, and naturally it was he who commanded the company rather than I, a recruit compared to him. He served on, amending his age from time to time, almost until the outbreak of the Second World War; he eventually had to be relegated to non-combatant duties, however, when the unit was mechanized, and he could not learn to ride a motor-cycle.

The men of Northumbria have soldiering in their blood, from their Scandinavian forebears, and from their ancestors who were constantly engaged in border warfare against the Scots. There was little difficulty in filling the ranks with part-time soldiers, and the local drill halls, situated in mining and agricultural villages, were used as community centres. All sorts of activities took place in them, such as dances, child welfare clinics and weddings, in addition to military training.

There was desperate unemployment in the early twenties, and many 'out of works' spent much of their time in these halls, hoping to pick up a few shillings from the quartermasters in return for cleaning rifles, limbers, and harness. The TA was the only hobby they could afford, and the annual training at the fourteen-day camps was their holiday. Ammunition boots were issued to them, which they wore constantly, whether in uniform or not, having no others.

At one annual camp my platoon sergeant remarked to me; 'We've aal had a bloody clarty time in France—noo lets aal enjoy oorsells withoot aal them flaming shells and bullets.'

They did, and on pay night, during camp, officers' picquets in GS wagons roamed the pubs of the nearest town, picking up the most intemperate and tenderly bringing them back to their tents.

The majority of officers were professional men or students like myself, not rich men as were many pre-war types, and we could only just afford to pay our expenses, such as mess bills, from the pay we received during the annual camps. During these periods of training, which took place at places like Catterick, Ripon, or Leyburn in Yorkshire, the captains and subalterns indulged in a great deal of ragging and horseplay. We were particularly addicted to chariot races in tin hip baths drawn by horses—a hazardous sport as the bottoms of the chariots became almost red hot, and the occupants were frequently decanted out of them at curves in the grass track.

On the guest night of a sister battalion, at a brigade camp, the subalterns raided all the other messes, picking up the brigadier and all the commanding officers, whom they threw into limbers and galloped round the area; they eventually deposited them altogether in one tent, bruised and sore, and restored them with liquor. I doubt if such conduct would be tolerated nowadays, but it should be remembered that these young officers had just survived a war in which subalterns' lives were brief, and they were inclined to rejoice in their survival.

Despite this playboy attitude of all ranks, the standard of training was quite good; and a visiting foreign military attaché was heard to remark that on manoeuvres he had difficulty in distinguishing Regular Army from Territorial personnel. Our standard of shooting on the ranges was quite high, and we had many marksmen good enough to compete at Bisley. There was one serious gap in the young officers' education—we were taught nothing of administration, since this was done by permanent staff; and our ignorance was a handicap when this staff was withdrawn at the outbreak of the next war. Most of my contemporaries passed with ease the examinations for promotion to captain and major, but these were limited to tactics (plus weapon handling for TA officers); the problems of pay, interior economy, and administration within their units were never touched upon.

During my years as a student I also found time, as any young man should, to do my courting. Soon after my return from the Rhine Army, I was visited by a brother officer from our battalion on the Western Front. He brought with him his new wife and her sister Lila, a petite miss with a little girl's face, which she still retains fifty years after our first meeting. She was wearing a black blouse, very becoming, and accidently *décolleté*, exposing a white round shoulder, and I was shot through the heart. Within a few days we were walking out, and within a few weeks we were engaged, although it was impossible to tell when we could marry as neither of us had any money—a handicap which we carried for most of our married life. Lila, who eventually

95

acquired the nickname of Penny, received few of those indulgences which an engaged girl might expect, as my student's grant came to only a few shillings a week, after I had paid some trifle to my mother for my keep. Our courting, therefore, was done during walks in the country, with occasional visits to the pictures, or in friends' houses. She never, then or afterwards, complained, so she must have decided that I was to be her man; and after fifty years she still seems to be of the same opinion.

I passed the final examination for the licentiate in dental surgery for the Royal College of Surgeons during March 1923. I was one of the first ex-service students to do so, because in a hazardous moment I decided to take two parts of the test during one visit to London. It was customary to take these separately, but I wanted to save the expense of two visits. When I returned, successful, to my dental hospital and had been congratulated by my fellow students, I got the impression that they felt I had beaten the starter's pistol. The dean, conveying his congratulations, added, 'They must have asked you something you knew', and I was reminded of the sarcastic schoolmaster at Rutherford College, who had been confounded at my passing matriculation ten years before. One of the professors, shaking me by the hand, said, 'Now you have qualified, your troubles are just beginning.'

He was too right!

My student's grant terminated immediately, and the only money I had was part of my war gratuity. At the present time, with all the advantages of the National Health Service, a newly qualified doctor or dentist may select from a number of well-paid appointments to begin his professional career. In the early twenties there were very few posts available, and there was no dole for professional people. The majority of the population could not afford to pay for dentistry, especially in the hard-hit North Country, and so few established practitioners could afford to employ an assistant; thus most of the young dentists of my year were very hard up for a few years. They were known as 'the hungry hundred'.

On 4th July, 1923, Penny and I got married, on nothing a year, and an overdraft at my bank of several hundred pounds, bought a house and put up a brass plate, hoping to build up a dental practice from scratch. The attempt to do so was a dead failure, for many reasons, the most important ones being lack of sufficient capital to wait five years, the usual time it takes to build a practice, and the prevailing poverty so few people could afford dental treatment, and there was no National Health Service in those days. After our son, Gerald, was born something had to be done to obtain an income. I could possibly at that time have obtained a commission in the Army Dental Corps, but I was not keen to give up the TA commission in my line regiment. After one or two applications, I was short-listed for an appointment in the School Dental Service in Surrey; I appeared before a committee at County Hall, Kingston-on-Thames, a little embarrassed because I had no morning suit like other candidates, this being the customary dress for applicants. I was given the post, mainly, I believe, because someone on the committee had been to Durham University and recognized my accent, and possibly because I looked very young and would be unalarming to child patients. The salary of £400 per annum seemed princely.

We moved to London suburbia and lived for some months in drab rooms, until we managed to rent a house. Housing was even more scarce than after the Second World War, and only my position as a county employee enabled me to be accepted as a tenant.

Now that I had an income, I was delighted to work hard in my profession, although the clinical work was done in extraordinary places. The School Dental Service at that time was the poor relation in all the services run by the local authorities; clinics and equipment were very meagre, even parsimonious, since little funds were made available from the rates. In my area in Surrey there were 22,000 schoolchildren, all of whom were potential patients; I operated in three centres—one in the crypt of a church, one in a room over a chemist shop, and one in the vestry of a parish church—when I could get into it, since when guests for weddings or funerals turned up, my patients had to be sent away.

There was no electrical equipment, and for many years the dentists worked with foot drills and extremely simple anaesthetic apparatus. Nevertheless, twice a week we regularly treated twenty to twenty-five patients who required 'gas' anaesthesia; I shudder to think of the risks both dentist and doctor took in doing so. However, this was good training for my future in the profession; since then I have had to practise in many strange places with very primitive equipment. In fact, looking back over the greater part of my professional life, I think that I have done clinical work under every adverse circumstance — except on ice.

Since I was still a member of the TA, I was attached to the 4th Queen's Regiment for normal training, and for some years I only saw my own unit at annual camp. But when I was approached by the adjutant of a neighbouring unit, the 44th Div. RASC, and asked if I would apply to join it, I made application and was accepted. The adjutant, Captain Buckle, thought that my service in infantry might be useful in helping to train his men in the use of small arms, an essential skill, since the service corps in any future war would need to take on a more combatant role than in former times. I have often been indebted to Denys Buckle, now Major-General Buckle, CMG, CB, during my army service, and am delighted that we still keep in touch.

In the RASC I probably learned more about the administration and organization of an army division than in any other unit in which I served; this was valuable when I went on senior officers' courses of instruction. Denys was also responsible for my promotion to brevet major, which in peacetime then was a great honour, normally leading to accelerated promotion.

The unit had recently been mechanized, but it still had a horsey flavour about it, as the commanding officer, Colonel Medcalf, was a horse lover. He was a rich bachelor, who looked and occasionally acted like a benevolent eighteenth-century sporting squire, being a square-shaped man with a ruddy complexion. His home or rather his country seat was a large mansion, complete with a ballroom, set in extensive grounds near Waltham Cross which at that time was almost rural. He lived there in solitary state and as servants were no problem in those days he did much entertaining, so his officers and their wives were occasionally invited to Sunday lunch. Though he was a wealthy man and knew that we were very poor he was never patronizing, and ensured that his guests were treated with every courtesy by his staff. The ladies were provided with a ladies' maid for the visit which sometimes embarrassed them as they were unaccustomed to such service. The luncheon parties were arranged like military operations, with exact timings for arrival, consumption of cocktails, the meal itself, retirement of the ladies after coffee, and their return in time to be conducted round the grounds and admire his horses and greenhouses. Afternoon tea round a blazing log fire was served at exactly four o'clock, and a whisky or sherry offered at five-fifteen which was the signal for departure, at five-thirty.

He spent his own money freely on his unit but never took to internal combustion engines instead of horses. His command was a happy one and though some thought him too old-fashioned to command in a mechanized army we looked up to him as a gentleman and regretted his departure. He had been a Territorial before the First World War, and he was most distressed when in the late twenties, he had to give up his command. So his officers arranged to dine him out in London, and to take him to whichever theatre show he wished to see. Being an old-fashioned man, he decided to see a performance in an Old Tyme Music Hall; and, to keep the farewell truly in period, everyone turned up in full evening dress, with opera hats and cloaks, and the mess president arranged to hire the last half-dozen hansom cabs still plying for hire in London. After dinner in a Vine Street restaurant, we mounted the cabs and clip-clopped through Piccadilly to the theatre, making an unusual sight for passersby. During the performance the stage manager came in front of the curtain and announced to the audience that the officers in the front stalls were saying farewell to their commanding officer, and that the orchestra would now play the march of the Royal Army Service Corps, 'Wait for the Wagon'. The announcement was well received, and the audience sang 'For He's a Jolly Good Fellow', although they did not know the colonel at all. He was a jolly good fellow, and I am glad that I had the opportunity of attending his dining-out party—and that I had a last opportunity of riding in a hansom cab.

Besides being an interesting hobby, TA soldiering had a social side to it which included the wives and sweethearts. An author, whose name I cannot remember, once wrote that a commission in the Territorial Army allowed one to mix with a higher society at a cheap rate. This was true, although one had to spend something on this hobby; certainly I had to provide myself with blue patrol uniform and mess kit out of my own pocket.

Now that our circumstances were improving, Penny and I had a wonderful social life, dining, dancing and visiting; and in the late twenties and early thirties, life was quite gay. There was a colour and pageantry in it which has never been regained since the Second World War. There were still rich countyfolk living comfortably on their estates, with servants and retainers, and on occasion they provided hospitality to officers encamped near their estates.

I recall being detailed to accompany my colonel and his adjutant on a visit to a titled gentleman and his wife, to take tea, followed by sherry. They lived in modest state, and the drawing-room was furnished in expensive Victorian elegance. Our hostess was a little old lady who looked, and was dressed like, 'the late dear Queen Victoria', whom she mentioned with affection. We sat rather shyly and uncomfortably on straight-backed chairs and were served with a delicate tea by what the old lady called 'her Abigail'; we exchanged small talk, commiserating with her—only from politeness—when she complained of fancied misdoings of servants and of the local populace. Then to our astonishment she addressed me directly, remarking sweetly and distinctly, apropos of nothing in particular, 'I do hate the lower orders, do you not, Major?'

In my surprise I nearly dropped my Limoges teacup,

choking on a toasted scone. My efforts to clear my throat were taken by the old lady as agreement, as she was slightly deaf, and she nodded as though approving my sentiments. This incident is still mentioned amongst my army friends, and it has never been decided if she was referring to anyone, including myself, in particular. Her husband was a cheery affable type, and when he called at our mess tent next morning to return our visit and was offered sherry or whisky, he replied, 'No thank you, I don't drink, it is far too early in the day, and I have had two already.'

One of the most interesting and picturesque duties of an officer holding a permanent commission was attendance at a King's Levée, when several hundred were introduced individually to the sovereign. Not everyone was so privileged, because the numbers were so large, and a command to attend usually depended on the wish of the honorary colonel of a regiment or corps. I attended two. The first, held by King George the Fifth shortly before his death, and another by the uncrowned Edward. Like debutantes' courts, levées have now ceased and passed into history, but I am glad to have taken part in a little of the pageantry for which our country is renowned.

Naturally, the officers to be presented had to be impeccably turned out, dressed in best service uniforms or in full dress, with medals and swords, so a great deal of kit was borrowed from elegant friends. The oft-quoted remark of a churlish field officer is worth repeating, 'Though I have never had the privilege of being presented to the sovereign myself, my top boots have been presented five times.'

On the first occasion, six officers of our unit were commanded to Buckingham Palace; and we assembled at Wilkinson's Sword Company shop in Pall Mall, where our turn-out was closely inspected by the honorary colonel and our adjutant. Several were directed to buy new articles of kit immediately, and as my spur straps were beyond regulation length, a cobbler trimmed them on the spot. We then walked to the palace, stared at by passersby, and were ushered into a large state-room full of service officers, judges, members of the Bar, and other presentees, all in uniform, robes, or court dress. Gentlemen ushers moved among the assembly, suggesting trifling adjustments to dress or accoutrements. It was a very colourful assembly; I had hardly time to take full note of it, before we were directed to file through some double doors which were guarded by gentlemen-at-arms holding pikes, who also carefully scrutinized everyone. They all held the rank of full colonel, or above, and checked any irregularities in dress; they stopped a scruffy looking subaltern (evidently not inspected by his adjutant), by crossing their pikes in front of him. He was terrified, and when one snapped at him, 'Your turnout is a disgrace to your regiment, leave the palace immediately. I shall communicate with your commanding officer', the lieutenant fled, blushing scarlet.

We filed through several state-rooms, and in the anteroom to the throne-room we were marshalled into single file and given our instructions:

'When tapped on the shoulder, walk through that open door for five paces, turn to your left, and bow to His Majesty. If he does not speak, turn right and march off out the opposite door.'

My turn came, and at exactly the same moment that I made my bow my name was called out by a chamberlain. I had time to notice that King George looked very ill, with a curiously waxen complexion, before I turned right and walked away to the open door as directed. It led to a wide staircase, on which Yeomen of the Guard were posted, who came to attention as every officer descended it. I remember wondering if there was a refreshment buffet, which there wasn't, and in a few moments I suddenly found myself in the courtyard where I joined my friends and the honorary colonel.

It seemed a sad anticlimax to see normal traffic passing a few yards away, after the pomp and ceremony inside the palace. However, the colonel took us all off to lunch at his club, which was a customary expense to honorary colonels after levées, and we had a good party.

These were halcyon days in the volunteer forces in the late twenties and early thirties; but soon we had to put aside all the pomp, fripperies and social dalliance, as Hitler's patience was becoming exhausted, and the more thoughtful of us began to realize that perhaps the thunderclouds of another great war were massing on the horizon.

Chapter 9

A MUSTERING OF SOLDIERS

DURING the decade 1920–30, war on any large scale was thought impossible by most of the population, who remembered the blood bath of 1914–18; and soldiers again became unpopular, reverting to their pre-war image of idle and dissolute men in the eyes of those who had not served in the armed forces.

As late as 1929 I remember taking an ex-subaltern of mine, who had joined the ranks and had now become penniless, into a public house near Victoria Station. He was in private's uniform and I in plain clothes, and the potman was reluctant to serve him, saying that soldiers were not welcomed as customers. I had to pull my rank on the publican and threaten to inform the licensing authorities before we got our drinks. Once when I was walking through Croydon in uniform, I was jeered at by a crowd of hoodlums who accused me of being the sort of person who started wars. About this time too, the Oxford Union passed the infamous resolution that 'never again will we fight for King and country' (although students were the first to volunteer when called); and newspapers and cinemas displayed pictures of the horrors of the Western Front — pronouncing 'Good-bye to all that'.

Fortunately for this realm of ours, a few thinking people, foremost of whom was Winston Churchill, realized that Nazi Germany was prepared to go to war if it could not obtain the objectives for its expansion by any other means; and the experts in the War Department began without much fuss or publicity to prepare for the defence of the country and Commonwealth. The establishments of units of the armed forces had been kept to a minimum to save expense; indeed funds for the training of Territorials had been cut to such an extent, that only selected personnel could be paid for all training courses. In about 1933, units were told that they should concentrate on recruiting, and more money was made available.

The most immediate and dangerous threat from Hitler, if he decided on hostilities would be the bombing of cities by aircraft; so first of all the War Ministry decided to raise a large anti-aircraft formation, and to educate the civilian population in air-raid precautions. The simplest way to raise this new force was to build on to existing Territorial units, changing their weapons from those of infantry and field artillery to searchlights and anti-aircraft guns. Many old TA infantry units were converted to Royal Engineers for this purpose; but none welcomed the change from their traditional rôle, especially as it meant changes in uniform and often in headquarters.

Some time in 1936 Brigadier Ogle, who was commanding an anti-aircraft brigade in Surrey, asked me if I would transfer in the rank of major and raise a company of searchlights at Hackbridge (near my home). This was to be part of the 31st Regiment Royal Engineers, which was formed from a famous old Territorial Unit, the 6th City of London Rifles. This battalion had fought long and hard on the Western Front during the First World War, but was now so much under strength that it was little more than a cadre. Its commanding officer, Lieutenant-Colonel Cannon, deplored the change, and also the introduction of new officers, especially senior ones, who were to assist in raising and training a different type of unit of nearly sixteen hundred men. I was accepted into the regiment a little reluctantly, and I feel sure that the brigadier had insisted on my transfer only because I lived in the recruiting area, was well known, and was likely to bring in recruits.

Transferred officers were given a small allowance to cover the cost of changes in uniform, badges, etc.; however,

I had to purchase the Royal Engineers mess kit and blue patrol uniform at my own expense, since the War Office had declared these non-obligatory, even though all TA officers were expected to possess them.

When I had been promoted to full field rank, I was the senior major in the regiment; but I spent my first fourteen days of annual training operating a searchlight with a detachment of young officers, which was a little strenuous but useful basic training for my new rôle in the army.

In some ways the atmosphere in the unit was not congenial, possibly due to discontent of the old riflemen at their change of rôle. I thought of resigning several times, but the brigadier dissuaded me from doing so, saying that the new formation would settle down soon.

Soon after I joined, the battalion moved from the old headquarters, Farringdon Road Drill Hall in the City of London, to North Surrey, where we occupied a fine new building at Stonecot Hill near Sutton. Two companies were raised there, and two others in temporary premises at Merton Park and in an old mansion at Hackbridge. I was appointed to command 327 Company, which was only in embryo at that time, consisting of four officers, about half a dozen NCOs and men, and Staff Sergeant Instructor Regan from the regular army. He was an efficient, taciturn soldier, and was instructed to recruit four hundred volunteers as quickly as possible. Scores of similar formations were being raised all over the British Isles at that time by amateurs like myself; and as we were given only trifling sums to help us to recruit, we had to dip into our own pockets for many necessities, such as a great deal of entertaining. Few of the officers appointed to my company had had previous military experience, like those hastily commissioned into units on the outbreak of the First World War, but they made up for this by their enthusiasm.

We put on our uniforms and visited public houses, picture halls, and British Legion clubs making recruiting speeches; and when we got a real searchlight, we took it round to any convenient open space and threw a beam up to the clouds to attract a crowd, which we harangued like street traders.

Although the populace was now taking some notice of the Nazi threat, they were not yet prepared for a war such as that of 1914–18; so at first we emphasized that we were a defence force rather than a belligerent outfit, and the recruits began to come in. Many were ex-soldiers, who brought their sons along with them to join; and many of them were ex-patients of mine who had been treated at my school clinic a few years before.

It was hard work at first, but after we had recruited the first fifty, men came by dozens to our headquarters asking to enlist.

By the spring of 1938 the company was nearly three hundred strong, and training became a problem. We had the bare minimum of training equipment, and only one or two NCOs. They had little experience of anti-aircraft duties, and so we had to arrange a crash course to train some instructors. I made it my duty to see and to swear in all recruits, making something of a ceremony of it; and if after consulting Staff Sergeant Regan I thought a man was intelligent and would make a good NCO, he was placed in a special squad, to be given intensive training by a regular instructor. Most of them did well, absorbed knowledge like sponges, and were given promotion within a few weeks. Many were officer material, and I think over eighty were commissioned during the Second World War, two of them becoming lieutenant-colonels. The rank and file came from all walks of life, and I look back upon this modest unit, 327 Company, as one of the finest collections of soldiers I have ever had the honour to command. All were keen and willing, and they good-humouredly put up with some serious handicaps, since builders were pulling down the old mansion over our heads for months. There was never any serious crime or indiscipline, and the company had an *esprit de corps* which continues to this day among ex-members.

We attended one annual training, still greatly under strength, when the RAF flew planes as targets for us; then, spurred on by high-ranking officers from Air Defence, we trained several times a week at our drill hall and over many week-ends. We were all engaged in our normal civilian occupations during the day, but most of us spent the evenings at military pursuits.

After many years of service as a part-time soldier, it is my firm belief that although England is not a military nation such as France or Germany, no other country can produce such an efficient volunteer reserve force like our Territorials so cheaply, or produce men who can learn the use of arms so quickly if they feel it necessary.

In 1936 my wife and I spent a holiday in Germany, and from my observations of the numbers of uniformed soldiers in the streets and of the belligerent attitude of the people, I felt that war was coming. The harbinger of war for me and my command was the Munich crisis.

During September 1938, the situation at our headquarters at Hackbridge was even more confused than usual. The builders were still pulling down bits of the old house, making alterations to rooms and preparing to build a proper drill hall on the kitchen garden, so most of our training had to be done in old stables or in the open. Men were rolling up to enlist in large numbers, and much time was taken up in filling up attestation papers and swearing in recruits. As most of our training up to then had been individual instruction in manning searchlights and Lewis guns, the company was not yet organized into sections and detachments; but fortunately a number of NCOs had been officially promoted after their intensive course under Staff Sergeant Regan. We had only three lights and three guns, so classes were crowded, but enthusiastic.

These volunteers who had come forward to defend their country hardly expected to be called upon to do so so soon, and it seems incredible that even officers had little information about the true political situation, except what they could pick up from newspapers. I can remember no conferences, or even confidential information, about what we should do if war was declared; we had only, as all units did during peacetime, a sketchy standing order which set out the procedure for calling up personnel in an emergency. A few men living near the headquarters were detailed as key men, and these could be warned within an hour to report immediately and to prepare the building and equipment before the bulk of the personnel arrived. All ranks had been warned to arrive at the drill hall, if called in emergency, with what kit they possessed, washing and shaving materials, and a day's food.

Owing to tight security, only a few senior staff officers could have been aware of the deployment of anti-aircraft units in case of a sudden emergency; I think that most of the officers in these units were in complete ignorance of the overall plan until the crisis was upon us. However, in the traditional English manner, we muddled through.

During September 1938 the Prime Minister, Mr Chamberlain, departed for Germany to hold conversations with Herr Hitler, and he tried to avert a European war by making a compromise on the subject of the Sudetenland, which was then part of Czechoslovakia. The news in the papers was so disturbing that even we part-time soldiers guessed that there must be a call-up soon, so I was relieved when my staff sergeant delivered a bulky brown envelope to me at my home saying that the adjutant had instructed him to do so immediately. It seemed obvious that it contained mobilization orders, but the envelope was sealed and marked 'secret not to be opened except by a company commander, and then only *after an order* from the commanding officer!' I hoped that I would receive this order soon, and I took the envelope with me to my school dental clinic in Carshalton.

Treatment of patients went on as usual, but nurses kept popping in to my surgery to ask me if I thought there might be a war. Not wishing to alarm them, I pooh-poohed the idea, but remarked that if one began we had it all buttoned up.

During the afternoon session, while I was engaged in filling the tooth of a reluctant toddler, our caretaker, very excited, rushed into the surgery and announced that a soldier on a bicycle was at the door asking for somebody called Major Peacock—could that be me? Guessing who the caller might be, I stepped out of the surgery. It was the staff sergeant from my HQ at Hackbridge, who said, 'Sir, I have orders to call out the key men and am just going out on my bike to do so.'

I told him that I would be at the drill hall in a few minutes and then returned to the surgery. Acting on the example of Drake who remarked on hearing news of the approaching Armada, 'There is time to finish the game and thrash the Dons too', I completed the filling for my patient, then I took off my white coat and told my nurse to apologize and dismiss the rest of the children and parents, as my services were needed elsewhere.

I then rang the County Hall; I got straight through to a senior clerk and told him that I was called up, and that the county would be short of a school dentist for an indefinite period. I heard him give a gasp of amazement, then he recovered himself and wished me good luck.

My drill hall was only half a mile away, and I arrived there in my car just in time to see the first of our key men arriving, dressed in a boiler suit and pedalling a bicycle as though in a race. On seeing Sergeant Regan at the door, he exclaimed, 'Here I am sir,' and then looked round as though he thought Germans might be lurking in the garden.

Regan gave him a list of names and said, 'Make yourself useful, lad, and call out all the men on this paper, and get yourself properly dressed before coming back.'

I had the unopened envelope in my hands and was just about to open it, when Regan remarked severely, 'I would not do that, sir, there is no word about mobilization, just key men, and it states you must wait for the CO's permission.'

Just then two double-decker London Transport buses drove furiously up to the door; an inspector jumped off one and rushed up to me panting, 'Here we are, sir. Do we leave the buses, and can the drivers go home? I was told to stop them in Tooting, put the passengers off, and drive here, taking no notice of speed limits.'

We were just as surprised as the passengers and drivers must have been, and having had no prior information I asked the inspector to wait a moment or two until I sorted things out. We managed to put a call through to the adjutant at Regimental HQ some miles away, and I remarked testily, 'Look you, I'm going to open this confounded secret envelope now, we haven't a clue this end of what the hell's happening.'

I could hear more buses arriving as the adjutant replied, 'I can't give you orders as the CO has not arrived, but candidly, old man, if I was in your position, I would do so and damn the consequences.'

So I opened it, and the staff sergeant and I pored over the contents. There was no mention of buses until nearly the end, under the heading 'transport', and, as we had surmised, they were to carry personnel; so we told the inspector that we had no troops yet, but that the drivers should park their vehicles, go home to calm their wives, and return in two hours with some food.

We then had to plan for the reception of the personnel should they be called up, and for their formation into troops and sections. We hit upon the simple plan of using a quarter-master's stores, where all items are kept in separate bins or compartments, and where a man who is being fitted out proceeds from one compartment to another receiving different items from each. We appointed section officers, and hoped that when they arrived they could make up their sections by drawing men from different compartments or rooms.

Now every man was supposedly trained for certain duties —drivers, spotters, light operators—so we arranged that men trained for the same rôle would be placed in different parts of the building as they arrived, and that the section officers would select men from each—six drivers, six spotters, six light operators, and so on. Having made up a full section, the officer would then assemble them and keep them together until he received further orders.

We had hardly time to make these arrangements, by sticking notices on the assembly points, when the adjutant rang, saying briefly, 'The balloon has gone up—carry on with your orders in the written instructions.'.

The first thing to do was to send the key men out through the district, like the bearers of fiery crosses gathering the clans. In the meantime I had written a note to the manager of the local cinema, asking him to put a slide on the screen announcing the call-up. As everyone else was busy, I stepped outside the drill hall grounds and flagged down a passing motorist, who was highly indignant. However, when I whispered the news and gave him the note, his attitude changed, 'God in heaven,' he exclaimed, 'war—you can depend on me, sir.'

He turned his sports car and shot off in the direction of the Odeon Cinema at Wallington.

By an odd chance Penny, my wife, was in the audience, and she was the only person there who was not astonished when the film was stopped and a notice appeared instead:

'All ranks of 327 Coy. 31st Searchlight Regiment will report immediately to the headquarters bringing all uniform and food for 24 hours.

Signed: B. Peacock, Major,
Officer Commanding

She simply said to herself, 'I'd better go home and pack his kit and cut some sandwiches.'

Our son Gerald, then a Boy Scout, delivered them to me at the drill hall within an hour.

The promptitude with which men reported to the drill hall was astounding; and with them came recruits, clamouring to enlist, but we could only refer them to Regimental HQ, since we had not time to deal with them. Our total strength at that time was about 12 officers and 350 other ranks, only half of which had any uniforms other than a khaki side cap, blue boiler suit and a kit bag. Many of them working locally appeared within the hour; our city gents arrived later in bowler hats, with umbrellas and briefcases, and were sent home to get what kit they had, returning very soon in motor-cars driven by their wives.

Fortunately the section officers were some of the first to arrive, and they immediately got on with selecting their NCOs and men, so Captain McCobe, my second-in-command, the sergeant major and myself were able to examine our orders in detail and to have a conference. We were to mobilize and proceed to an area near Ware in Hertfordshire, and to deploy detachments on sites indicated by map references.

It seems odd that a unit located in southern suburbia should be sent to battle positions in Hertfordshire, for it meant traversing London and none of us knew the area. However, miraculously, maps arrived from the adjutant and the picture became clearer.

At close intervals private lorries and trucks arrived at the drill hall, and soon we had enough to equip each section with some form of transport; since most officers and some NCOs had their own cars, we thought we would use these for communications, hoping the government would pay for them some time later. Although we grumbled and groused at our tardy information, we had to recognize that a great deal of excellent staff work had been done at a high level; at no time were we entirely nonplussed through lack of administrative arrangements.

I had entered a practically empty drill hall at 16.30 hours, and by 20.30 hours I was able to report to the adjutant that two sections were ready to move and the remainder were waiting for some extra transport. I sent off my second-in-command, Captain McCobe, and Captain Surridge, with some HQ staff and the two troops, with orders to report at Battle Headquarters and do some preliminary reconnaissance. It was one of the greatest moments of my life as I watched them drive off, wondering what was to be the end of it all.

The drill hall now seemed strangely empty of men, and I wondered where they had gone, since, according to our nominal rolls, nearly all the men had reported and been allotted to a section; then Sergeant Regan, who in our early days had a poor idea of part-time soldiers, remarked with his usual astuteness, 'A hundred to one they are all in the Red Lion pub opposite—what about trying a bugle call, sir?'

Our bugler, who owned his own instrument, was an elderly gentleman who had finished his regular army service before the First World War, so we could only guess at his age. He was only too delighted to show what he could do, and he blew the alarm, the fall-in, and all the other calls in his repertoire, causing great consternation in the neighbourhood. The pub doors opened and the bulk of 327 Company emerged in some panic and sprinted back to the drill hall, where the sergeant major greeted them with some well-chosen words.

By 21.30 hours we were on the move, en route for Ware, with only six absentees, who had been away from home that day and joined us later; a very creditable mustering of civilian soldiers. We arrived at the map reference at which our headquarters was to be sited and found, as stated in orders, a telephone junction box on a telegraph pole at the side of a field. There was nothing else on the site, no cover or accommodation; and once we had erected a searchlight and an anti-aircraft Lewis gun, there was little we could do except to send the sections off to their areas to fend for themselves.

The telephone connected only with Air Defence HQ on some airfield, thus we were quite isolated from Regimental HQ fifteen miles away. So I approached the local vicar in his parsonage and obtained permission to station a telephonist by his phone. He and his wife were quite co-operative, but they insisted on the soldier removing his muddy boots and wearing a pair of slippers. My second-in-command knocked up a nearby publican and got the men under cover in some outhouses, and actually secured a bedroom for me. The pub was called The Crooked Billet, and had probably had soldiers billeted in it in the seventeenth century, before barracks were built. Our stay was very profitable to the landlord, who could rarely have had so much custom as we provided. Despatch riders from the sections, riding their own machines, reported that all was well, and that the detachments were on their sites under cover in barns and farmhouses.

During the night we received a despatch ordering us to draw equipment and arms from the mobilization store at Buntingford, and Captain Surridge arrived there at 08.00 hours. To his astonishment the place was closed and shuttered, and only after hammering at the doors and windows did he raise a sleepy caretaker, who said indignantly that this depot never opened for business before half past nine. As there were no other members of the staff present, Captain Surridge's party could only wait until they turned up, as it was evident that the news of pending hostilities had not yet penetrated to the mobilization store. When the staff did arrive, several other units were clamouring for their arms; but Surridge made such a fuss that he obtained ours in bulk, and in the confusion he managed to sign for them unchecked. This was just as well, since for years afterwards when I was plagued about missing binoculars, watches, etc., I persisted in replying to demands for payment that no check had been done at the time of issue, adding that my men had been hoicked out of their civilian jobs at a moment's notice, had had no sleep, and were extremely incensed that civilian employees of the army staff had been unprepared for us.

We received a few tents, and a marquee for use as a company HQ, and, to our surprise, our full complement of searchlights and arms, and prepared ourselves to resist the might of the Luftwaffe, if they came. No rations had been issued, but everyone received ration money on a generous scale. A bank account had been opened in Ware for my company, and from this we drew funds for pay, and a £5 bounty for each man given on call-up. Money was one thing we were not short of, and my ex-soldiers look back on that mobilization as a time of plenty, when they had more money in their pockets than ever before or since. They fed in local cafés and pubs, and fed well; however, their clothing and boots were a problem, since most of them stood about for days in the rain, in muddy fields, wearing civilian shoes and clothes.

On 27th September, we received a message to prepare for air co-operation exercises. Everyone believed that this meant operation against German planes, and we all looked forward to it; however, it rained and blew that night, and it would have been impossible for us to engage any planes, friendly or otherwise. The marquee blew down and nearly suffocated the signallers underneath the canvas. The brigadier turned up and, thoughtful as ever, laid on a rum ration for everyone; which, however, necessitated Captain McCobe driving over 150 miles to collect and distribute it.

The return of Mr Chamberlain from Munich, waving the historic piece of paper signed by himself and Herr Hitler on 29th September, was an anticlimax to our exertions, and we all felt that the Luftwaffe had let us down. It is just as well, for our keenness and willingness would not have been enough to engage it skilfully; but by the time we received orders to stand down, return our equipment and arms to store, and go back to our homes, we had learned a great deal. As Mr Chamberlain remarked, 'Hitler has missed the bus', for when we assembled again for actual war, we did so without fuss or excitement, and we were well trained.

Within ten days of the call-up, I was back in my clinic, having laid aside my revolver and taken up my forceps again. The affair had one fortunate outcome, as shortly afterwards I was appointed the Senior Dental Officer for Surrey, directing the work of all dentists and dental nurses on the staff; perhaps the County Health Committee thought my military activities fitted me for issuing directives. Later, I discovered that it was much easier to command a regiment of soldiers than two score of professional men, each an individualist.

I look back with amusement to our mobilization for Munich, and with a certain degree of pride. It was done well because of the civilian soldiers themselves, because of their keenness, their commonsense, their willingness to put up with rough conditions without any grousing, and particularly their good humour. They all declared that they had enjoyed themselves.

A few weeks later, the Lord Mayor of London and the Corporation gave a splendid reception for the officers of the 1st Anti-Aircraft Division who had taken part, and for their wives. It was held in the Guildhall, and Penny and I look back on that function as the most lavish and colourful we have ever attended. Our hosts were all in full regalia, every officer guest was in mess kit, and the ladies in magnificent ball gowns. There were several bars and buffets serving champagne and expensive delicacies, and we danced to the music of Marius Winter's famous band. There was a concert and a card room for non-dancers, and the string band of the Honourable Artillery Company played selections. Gog and Magog in the main hall looked down on a colourful assembly, which must have been like that at the ball in Brussels prior to Waterloo. During the last waltz, while the band played the 'Eton Boating Song' and several hundred couples were on the floor, Penny and I stood to one side to stare and to memorize the wonderful spectacle, which would probably be impossible to repeat nowadays when the old decorative uniforms have almost disappeared. For me, this entertainment was the end of what I have called 'The Long Furlough' — the years between the wars.

MIDDLE AGE
AT WAR

Chapter 10

'AUX ARMES, CITOYENS!'

FEW people connected with the armed services believed that Mr Chamberlain's piece of paper, signed by the Führer and himself, would result in a lasting peace in Europe, we knew it would only delay the start of actual hostilities.

Certainly the War Office had no illusions, they poured out money for the manufacture of munitions of war. Air Defence High Command urged the citizen soldiers to undergo more intensive training, and to bring in more recruits. We were directed to concentrate on arms training, cutting out even elementary squad drill and roll-call parades; I once received a rocket from a visiting general because I had the company formed up to greet him before they started individual instruction. At the same time, senior officers, colonels and above, unreasonably expected that the men should be smartly turned out, and be able to present arms to them like trained soldiers; and I must confess that we had hidden away a small group of ex-soldiers who could be produced in an emergency to form a quarter guard and pay proper compliments to those who were entitled to them. Much was expected of the citizen soldiers, and all responded willingly. From the time of Munich most of the officers and senior NCOs devoted almost as much time to their military duties as to their civilian occupations, and to some of us our civilian work became secondary.

Arms and equipment came tumbling into our head-quarters, so much of them that we had to employ some permanent staff to service and maintain them, as there was little time for the part-time soldiers to do so. Uniforms were still scarce, and some of our men even went to war wearing civilian overcoats and boots. During the latter part of 1938, our collection of amateurs, all volunteers, turned into a company of soldiers nearly five hundred strong; and even Staff Sergeant Regan, a man of faint praise at any time, remarked after a successful week-end exercise, 'You now have a real company to command, sir, instead of a lot of odds and sods.'

The regiment was now commanded by Lieutenant-Colonel Harvie Watt,* a barrister and a TA officer, who had been posted to the unit some time before as second-in-command from a regiment of Royal Engineers.

We were called up again in July 1939 for a month's intensive training, which was called 'Partial Manning of Air Defences', over the area of Surrey and Sussex which was to be our battle station in case of war. It gave us a wonderful opportunity to complete our organization, and to test our communications with various headquarters and with the RAF Operations Centres which directed our actions. Our company dealt with Kenley and Biggin Hill aerodromes, important fighter stations for the defence of London. After the first few days the ancillary and supply services of the anti-aircraft division began to function, and we operated as though on active service. Some huts had been built in a pasture near Godstone for company HQ staff, and most of the troops who were dispersed on searchlight sites were in tents. We still had a lot of civilian vehicles, and officers and men used their own cars and motor-cycles, for which they received a small allowance and free petrol. They needed them, too, for our deployment covered most of the county of Surrey. The weather was favourable for anti-aircraft training and we did well, picking up targets flown for us by the RAFVR pilots; and we felt that if war came we were now reasonably prepared for it.

When we stood down and dispersed, the commanding officer left for South Africa on business, and I took my wife and son, Gerald, to Paris for a few days' holiday. On our second day there I picked up a newspaper, and although I

* Later Brigadier Sir George Harvie Watt, QC, TD, DL, etc.

am no French scholar, it seemed to me that the news was pretty grim. The streets were full of young soldiers who looked as though they had just been called up for service, and I put a few questions to a group of them who were drinking in a café. Their answers decided me to get in touch with my drill hall immediately. By great good luck I got through on the telephone as quickly as though from my home. A dull clerk answered, and told me that all was quiet, nothing doing; and I was just about to ring off when he said, 'Of course the key men are here,' and then, as an afterthought, 'The brigadier has just come in, would I care to speak to him?'

I said something brisk, and told him to put the brigadier on the line. He spoke, 'That you, Peacock? Where are you? Paris!—right, get back immediately, you will have to take command in the colonel's absence and most likely mobilize the regiment.'

We packed hurriedly, caught an evening train and the night boat, and arrived at Newhaven, where I had left my car, in the early hours of the morning. There had been no opportunity to get any food on the journey, but driving up towards London I noticed a TA camp at Forest Row in Sussex, and I made myself known to the commanding officer, who had just had startling news about the situation. He very kindly laid on breakfast for Penny, Gerald and me in his mess, and we set off again, arriving home at about 09.00 hours. I rang up the regimental HQ and spoke to the adjutant, who said he was expecting the key word for mobilization at any moment, adding, 'everything is under control,' and that I might as well pack my kit and arrange my affairs before taking up command. By the time I had got into uniform and had a discussion with Penny, he rang again, saying, as he had done for Munich, 'The balloon's gone up, everything functioning.'

I had a quick shufti around the outlying companies, including my own, and I was a little disturbed that the men were not coming in as quickly as I thought they had done previously. I need not have worried, for many of them had run down to their war positions in their own cars and quietly taken over equipment and huts from a unit just pulling out. Regimental HQ was near Horley, and as the companies were soon functioning without any necessary direction from me, I drove down there and found the quartermaster and a few other bods already established in a small hutted camp. As regimental commander I found I had much less to do than as a company commander, for companies were self-accounting units, and the adjutant seemed able to cope with most problems. So my job was general supervision, which meant driving over long distances to visit the companies which were spread out over two counties. All seemed well with them, and I was able to report to the brigadier that we were ready.

Oddly enough, it was a few days later in a police station, which I was visiting on some liaison business, that I heard Mr Chamberlain's speech in which he announced that we were at war, and I heard the first air-raid warning as I drove back to camp. Nothing happened for several days, for what is now called the 'phoney war' had begun, so I arranged for Penny and Gerald to visit me. Penny stayed in a local pub, and I took Gerald into my hut. In the middle of the night I heard a racket outside, and then to my astonishment the adjutant, wearing his gas mask, came into my quarters mumbling something about a gas alarm. I shall never forget my son's first words as he awoke—he was only fourteen—'Shall I put on my gas mask now, Dad, or wait till you do?'

With a pang, I began to hate war, I had never thought it would apply to children.

The adjutant had sensibly got all personnel wakened and turned out, wearing their respirators, awaiting instructions. I remembered the words in the Gas Training Manual: 'It is the duty of the senior soldier present to test for gas.' So, putting only the mouthpiece of my mask in position, I emerged from my hut, and a little tentatively I sniffed the air. I was told recently by an ex-soldier who had been there that I remarked irritably, 'The only bloody things I can smell are fresh air and perspiration—take off your masks. Who rang that gas alarm?'

A doltish man on sentry duty, probably the only person awake at the time, had done so, and to this day we have not discovered why, or if he even knew himself.

Things went along quietly for a few days; the only singular occurrence was the arrival of one of our majors, a company commander, who from his martial appearance looked like a Guards officer, asking to be relieved of his command as he found the strain too great and his civilian employers would like him back at work. I told him to return to his company and to make another request to the commanding officer when he returned from abroad.

An odd bod wearing curious trousers and a blue patrol jacket appeared unannounced and said he had been detailed as our chaplain; he then immediately asked to be provided with an official car, a driver/batman, quarters and several other things. As we were all using our own cars and were short of men at Regimental HQ, I refused; but he was not happy, so I sent him to visit the companies and to stay a few days with each, as we had no flock for him at headquarters. Oddly enough, he obtained one of the first official cars we received, and immediately, without asking my permission, he departed on leave to Norfolk, taking the car and driver. He soon got posted away.

After the first few days of mobilization, for some weeks we had a very quiet war, and most of our problems were administrative, such as arranging for men to have baths at local authority establishments and to have their clothes laundered. Though extra transport soon arrived and we could dispense with our own motor-cars and motor-bikes, uniforms were still very scarce, and until much later so were ammunition boots. It was almost winter before all the men were equipped with them and given the new battledress. Shortly after one detachment received their issue, they were visited by General Pile, who was commanding all the anti-aircraft troops in Great Britain. He asked a corporal of my company, an educated, rather precise man, if the soldiers preferred them to service dress; and he received the reply, 'Sir, in this detachment of mine they are looked upon with great disfavour.'

'There,' said the general turning to me, 'the whole army is old-fashioned apparently except myself. You must get modernized—impress this on all ranks: this war is not going to be old-fashioned.'

How right he was.

We had expected the Luftwaffe to appear in force almost immediately, but except for the occasional plane which we thought to be on a reconnaissance flight nothing happened; we felt the war to be an anticlimax after all the trouble we had taken to prepare for it. It was like attending an annual camp that was open to receive visitors. The first was our honorary colonel, Harold Mitchell, MP, a kindly, generous gentleman, whose first words to me were, 'You will need money—money is always useful,' and he handed me a handsome cheque for over a hundred pounds, adding, 'Use this as you think fit.'

I immediately informed the company commanders to draw on this for necessities not provided by the army authorities. He was delighted when I drove him about the country to visit our sites, and he seemed very pleased with all he saw. Oddly enough, I have not seen him again, to this day.

Within a few days we were asked to provide a draft of officers and men for service in France as an observer unit, the first of many. Most of our volunteer soldiers had expected to serve throughout the war in the regiment they had first joined, and we were always sorry when men were drafted away, but this is often a necessity in wartime.

Colonel Harvie Watt had difficulty in obtaining a passage from South Africa back to England, and he eventually arrived by flying boat from Beira, a fortnight after mobilization. He came to headquarters within a few hours, and after telephoning to my second-in-command I returned to my company. When I arrived at Godstone, in addition to the quarter guard turned out for my inspection, there was also an unofficial one, parading in the background, made up of cooks and batmen, with an imitation field-gun made from cartwheels and a drainpipe, which fired a salute with fireworks. There was always a certain informality about 327

Company off parade, which gave it character, and for which I loved it; there was never any disrespect and practically no indiscipline for me to deal with. The men dealt with offenders privately, and it was not until after the war, at reunions, that I learned about incidents in which individuals had been disciplined by their comrades. One little incident illustrating the spirit of these civilian soldiers sticks in my mind, and I recall it with pleasure. I had picked up in my car three men going on leave, to give them a lift to the railway station, when we saw another man in uniform walking along the road. I asked, 'Is this one of ours?' and received the reply, 'Certainly not, sir.'

'How do you know,' I said.

'He would be a damn sight better turned out if he was in our mob, sir.'

During the winter of 1939-40 the anti-aircraft troops, always ready for action, always on exposed sites manning their guns and searchlights, were probably harder worked in rougher conditions than any others in England; one of our problems was to keep them from becoming ill after exposure to hard, wet and snowy weather, but there were few grumbles. During part of that time, I was dispatched on a senior officers' course at Sheerness for six weeks, which was nothing to do with anti-aircraft duties, but involved the handling of an infantry division. We roamed the countryside in deep snow, and the course became a test of stamina. Fortunately, because of my previous service in the infantry, I was able to cope with the curriculum, and I received a fair report before returning to my regiment.

After the news of the fall of France, which we received with surprising calm, we prepared to tackle enemy paratroops and possible invasion, so we concentrated on weapon training and digging little redoubts near our sites. Our instructions were to fight where we stood, and every man had his post. There was nothing wrong with morale, and I remember with deep feeling my old batman, Lance Corporal Cottingham, who had served even before the First World War—his age doubtful, but probably sixty—saying to me, 'You know, sir, I cannot march or run very much, but I am a crack shot—just show me my firing place, give me some extra ammunition, and I'll just stay there.'

A strange and rather comic episode occurred at about this time. One afternoon I received a curious signal from Regimental HQ: 'Prepare to receive ninety-six taxi cabs which will report to you at 18.30 at the Kings Head, Godstone—further instructions follow.'

We thought it a joke, but my second-in-command and myself stationed ourselves outside the pub; and, sure enough, the first London taxi cab chugged up, and the driver, touching his hat, said, 'Where to, sir?'

We directed him to our camp a couple of miles away, and did the same for the other taximen who arrived every few minutes. Further instructions were delivered from HQ, which stated that one cab should be sent to each searchlight site, and that if the driver was willing to stay he should be taken on as a civilian employee, otherwise he should return with his expenses paid. Some stayed, and I well remember one grey-haired old taxi driver saluting and declaring, 'Ex-sergeant of dragoons sir—I think I could be useful.'

He stayed and enjoyed himself with a detachment which was doing most of the cooking and other chores. A Lewis gun was mounted on each cab, and the vehicles were used for reconnaissance and detailed for counter-paratroop duties if necessary. The troops had a delightful time scouring the countryside and the pubs for miles around. We had one alarm that paratroops were landing, and a mobile column from company HQ left our camp in minutes like a fire brigade, and drove fifteen miles in misty weather to discover that it was misinformation from a nervous Home Guard sentry.

Later, during the Battle of Britain, one of our section headquarters was visited by Sir Winston Churchill, and he was received there by my second-in-command, Captain Surridge. The site was being used to test rockets and other novelties, and a staff of very senior officers who were accompanying the Prime Minister were anxious to demonstrate them. The great man was tired and ill-tempered after much travel, and he grunted, 'I invented most of them,' and sat in his car putting on a pair of slippers.

The atmosphere was tense until my captain tentatively asked him if he would care to take a drink of whisky. 'That,' said Churchill, 'is the only sensible suggestion I have heard all day.'

A double whisky was speedily poured from the officer's bottle, consumed hastily, with thanks; and the eminent visitors departed into the night.

One of the most irritating differences between this war and the previous one was the number of non-combatant specialists who visited us. Welfare officers, catering officers, entertainment officers, training experts, and even sewage engineers, most of them having been given temporary field rank with no previous army service, all of whom came to occupy our time and consume our drink. They usually arrived unannounced, and expected everyone to drop what he was doing and to attend to them immediately. I remember on one occasion keeping an impatient, rude, Catering Corps officer waiting for ten minutes, since I was engaged in dealing with a man on a charge; the result was a 'fizzer' from division, because he found that one of our cooks had thrown away some gristle of beef into a swill tub. He never said what we should do with it. They rarely did an actual job except to give advice, and we were left to do the work. In the old days, padres did welfare, and did it well, without much bothering combatant commanders; in this war, although there was an enormous hierarchy and establishment of welfare officers, I cannot recollect a case of difficulty which was not finally settled by battalion officers. The men preferred to talk with their own officers, rather than with strangers. In well-established units there is, or should be, a family atmosphere, and although there may be internal squabbles, members of it are usually loyal to each other.

I remember one of our ATS girls, who was unmarried but had become pregnant, asking to speak to me just before she was discharged. She saluted and said, 'Sir, I do not wish to leave your company without telling you that it is *not* one of *your* men who has got me into trouble and I am sorry to leave as it has been very pleasant working here.'

I felt that this was very thoughtful of her when she was

in such distress, and I thanked her sincerely for her remarks and for her loyalty to 327 Company.

One evening during the summer of 1940 I was handed a copy of battalion orders by my orderly officer, who had just read them and was looking surprised. One item was a list of personnel to be posted away from the regiment to a training centre as a cadre which would eventually form a new unit, and I was astonished to see my name heading it; I had had no warning that I would be included in the draft. This was the most unexpected and the saddest posting I ever received during my service, as it meant I was to leave a body of soldiers which I had recruited almost individually and had succeeded in training to a standard which satisfied inspecting officers. The posting was a surprise to nearly everyone else as well, and I took it hard since only a few of my own NCOs would accompany me. At first I thought of querying the order, but I then remembered the motto of my former regiment, the Old Fifth of Foot, *Quo Fata Vocant* — where the Fates call — and decided not to. This posting changed the whole pattern of both my military and my civilian career, and after this the Fates called me to many strange places and hazards.

While I was collecting the cadre at my own headquarters, Brigadier Ogle called to say that he was sad that I was leaving his command; he passed me a few compliments on my work in the formation of the unit, which softened the blow, and he wished us all good luck. Within a few days we were ready to move, and just before I handed over command to Captain Surridge there was a last ceremonial parade of all the NCOs and men who could be spared from the searchlight sites. Everyone on parade did their utmost to drill perfectly and to make it a memorable occasion, and I left the parade ground almost in tears.

The cadre of officers and men travelled to Hereford, and we joined a training depot at Bradbury Barracks, where we were promptly transferred to the Royal Regiment of Artillery. Thus I made my fifth change of cap badge and buttons since I first joined the army in 1916.

All ranks were redrilled, and I spent some days doing squad and arms drill in the ranks with my men. We were given a refresher course in the use of searchlights, under some instructors who were less experienced than ourselves; then three hundred conscripts were handed over to us to train and to organize into a battery. Several weeks later we marched out as such, still very raw, as we had spent some valuable time picking hops, since no other labour was available. Nevertheless, we were complimented as being the best battery raised in the depot; and although I had not recovered from my distress at being posted away from my original unit, I was slightly mollified at the notification that I had been awarded 90 per cent of marks for military knowledge and efficiency.

We joined a newly formed regiment in Hertfordshire, with HQ at Hemel Hempstead, and took over battle positions round about Hatfield. We were soon in action, when some German bombers attacking London approached it from the north, this being a less dangerous route than from the south and east. We had some excitement when some of our sites were bombed and machine-gunned from the air; but soon the weather turned foggy, and we sat for weeks idle except for administrative chores and became rather miserable.

However, just before Christmas 1940, I was appointed second-in-command of the regiment and went to live at Regimental HQ. Our commanding officer, Lieutenant-Colonel Hick, was a charming man who had served in the First World War as a Territorial officer and gained three decorations; he made me very welcome, and I thoroughly enjoyed serving under him; but my stay with his regiment was brief.

We were sitting at dinner one evening in Regimental HQ when the adjutant was called to the phone; when he returned he announced that I was detailed for foreign parts — in the tropics — and must report to Woolwich depot within three days. Everyone was surprised, especially Colonel Hick, who said, 'I'm going to see about this — surely division can send a younger man than you — you have done your stint.'

It turned out that a substantive major was required, and

I was probably the only one in the division who had held the rank before the war. Again I remembered the old motto, and I told the colonel that I thought he should not query the order, since this might make us both unpopular.

By an extraordinary chain of circumstances this decision, though leading to some strange and dangerous experiences, saved my life. Later in the war, Colonel Hick and nearly every officer and man from that Regimental HQ were killed during the Normandy landings; and I, after many hazards, returned safely home.

I sadly packed my kit, helped by my batman, Gunner Lewington, another pre-1914 soldier, who begged to come with me. I said no, that he, like me, had done his stint, and I knew he had even been in India in 1912 or thereabouts. He persisted and remarked, 'You know, sir, when I heard you was detailed for the East, something clawed at me — once you have seen the jungle it always calls you back.'

He was quite right, as I discovered for myself later, but I am glad that I refused to try to take him with me, as I feel he would not have survived. During his early life he had been on a training ship, so later he was posted to man a gun on a cargo boat, and at over fifty did a great job shooting at a U-boat in the Atlantic.

Once more there were sad farewells, and to my pleasure and surprise a presentation watch from the men whom I had brought from my original unit. My batman came with me to my home, and I remember we finished off all the drinks we could find in the sideboard, since it was unlikely that I should be available to consume them myself for a few years. Penny was now nursing in the north, and Gerald was at Barnard Castle School in County Durham; the house had suffered some damage from the bombing, and it felt empty and very deserted.

My army driver dropped me at the Woolwich depot of the Royal Artillery, and a new life began.

Chapter 11

TROOPING TO THE TROPICS

THERE is something very attractive about the historic old barracks at Woolwich with their colonnaded Georgian façade overlooking the immense parade ground, so I looked forward with interest and pleasure to living there for a time. However my first contact with one of the staff was neither welcoming nor pleasant. As frequently happens in army postings, the receiving unit had not yet had notice of my arrival; and when I reported to the officers' wing, the major in charge, a brusque, untactful officer, remarked sharply, 'Who are you, and what is your rank?'

As I was wearing a major's insignia, I felt a little niggled and pointed it out to him. 'You will have to take that down,' he continued. 'What I want to know is your real rank—everyone entering the depot must come down to permanent rank.'

He seemed disappointed to discover that mine was permanent, and pre-war, and he snapped, 'I suppose you must be one of these bloody Territorials.'

Obviously he did not want me about the place, and he sent me on leave for a few days until my papers and orders came through.

When I returned to the depot, I found that I was to conduct a draft of sixteen officers and 250 men to the tropics. Happily, one Major Arthur Stiby was an old friend of mine from the 4th Queen's Regiment; but the remainder were a curious mixture, and some were obvious throwouts who had left their regiments for their regiments' good. Immediately I appeared, six officers asked to be taken off the draft; one said that his wife was pregnant; another that for business reasons it was essential he stay in England; and a third that as a married man he should not be posted abroad. The others had frivolous reasons, and I was surprised, but not disappointed, when they did dodge the draft. The rank and file were mainly conscripts of three months' service, unenthusiastic, but prepared to do their job.

Our time at Woolwich was taken up with kitting out the men and ourselves with tropical outfits, and with a few exercise parades. The officers received a tropical uniform allowance of £20, except myself, since the paymaster stated that I should have bought this out of my original uniform grant when I was first commissioned in 1917; so I had to equip myself for service in the tropics at my own expense, and I never recovered the cost.

For some weeks, the Woolwich area was plagued with repeated, intense air raids, and several times during our stay the famous parade ground in front of the mess was littered with incendiaries. One of these was picked up by a small girl, who handed it to me, saying, 'Mr soldier, you should have this.'

It was a dud, and I threw it as far away as possible on to the grass and chased her home.

When we were at last ready to move, we were given a few days draft leave, and I managed to visit my parents in Newcastle to say farewell. They were both very aged; my mother hardly realized I was leaving; but my father, lying very tired and weak in bed, perked up when I quoted, knowing it would please him, 'I go to Philippi,' and he capped it, 'If we do meet again, why, we shall, smile. If not, why then, this parting was well made.'

I never saw my parents again.

I also managed to visit Gerald at school to tell him that he would have to be the man in the family, and to look after his mother; and I am proud to record that he did, until he too joined the RAF and was posted abroad. Penny came back home to Wallington for my last few days in England;

we said good-bye at Victoria Station, and she was left solitary for nearly four years, during which time she served in the WRNS and as a Red Cross nurse.

Orders to move my draft from Woolwich were brief and confidential, so brief that few of our officers believed that I was not better informed than they were. We were ordered to entrain at Woolwich Station at midnight for an unknown destination, although we guessed Liverpool or Southampton, to embark for service in a tropical climate. We assembled at 20.30 hours in a barrack room, and I was standing on a table giving a sort of pep talk, when an intense air raid began. The blackout screens on the windows were blown in, and I nearly fell off my dais. The bombing was so bad that we decided to dribble the men to the station in small groups commanded by officers, at intervals. Later, I discovered that we nearly had a deserter, and he an officer; but two others, unbeknown to me, kept him under surveillance, expecting him to abscond. He did not, but he had taken a lot of drink to brace himself.

My party crossing the parade ground last of all, had to kick burning incendiaries out of the way, as buildings close by were being struck by high explosive bombs. One of the parties barely escaped annihilation when a public house was hit just as they were approaching it. The landlord, miraculously unhurt, rushed out and shouted, 'Take anything you can carry, lads, before anyone else gets it.'

We were soon entrained and sat uncomfortably in our places hoping that the station itself would not be hit. After some delay we steamed off slowly in the direction of London; however, we did not cross the river, but set off to the south.

Early next morning when there was enough light to see the countryside, someone recognized that we were approaching Liverpool, probably having been routed through Oxfordshire. We detrained and marched to the docks through drab streets, where some men of the draft had their homes, so that their relatives had an unexpected last meeting with them.

The docks had had a pasting from the Luftwaffe the night before, but our ship, the *Duchess of York*, was intact, with nearly two thousand troops already aboard. Within an hour she cast off, and we sailed to join a large convoy of merchant ships under the escort of a cruiser, HMS *Glasgow*, and several destroyers, which was assembling off the Firth of Clyde. The weather was cold, grey and misty, so we saw little of the other ships in the convoy until we reached warmer latitudes; but one vessel stood out from the others: a magnificent Dutch liner, the *Willem Ruys*.

Ours was a crowded ship, and as it had been built for North Atlantic crossings, it was not very suitable for cruising in the tropics. Adequate ventilation, especially with all portholes closed, was almost impossible. The soldiers were crammed between decks and slept in hammocks touching each other; the air was foul, and at times it stank so much that it turned one's stomach, even when the sea was calm. In rough weather when men were seasick the sleeping quarters were almost unbearable. After a few days of this, hundreds of men slept on deck, despite rain or cold weather. Most of the officers were in cabins, where extra bunks had been installed. Arthur Stiby and I were most fortunate to have a tiny one to ourselves, but because the portholes were closed at night and due to lack of ventilation, we never slept in comfort; and when we reached the tropics we, too, often slept on deck.

However, all ranks had one unaccustomed luxury — magnificent food, and more than enough. The ship had been victualled abroad, so that there were no shortages; and the officers were astonished on the first night to be presented with a printed menu, similar to that produced in liners in peacetime, from which they could select four- or five-course dinners. Being one of the most senior army officers aboard, I was placed at the captain's table, where the food and service were beyond reproach. The soldiers in their messes received so much unaccustomed meat, eggs, bacon and bread, that within a few days they could not eat it. In England, eggs were limited to about one per week per person, but on that ship the men could have as many as three for breakfast, until they sickened of them. Beer and other drinks were rationed, but they were available in adequate quantities and were sold at reasonable prices, as were cigarettes. Smoking, or striking a light, was forbidden on deck during hours of darkness because of the danger of detection by German submarines; and a culprit if caught received dire punishment.

To avoid the dangers of submarines, the convoy was routed via the North Atlantic, almost to Iceland; we then made a wide circuit and approached Freetown in West Africa from the west. Before the ships had cast anchor, the locals swarmed out in canoes and bum-boats offering us souvenirs, drink, and their sisters in the same breath; and they added every swear word in the English language, so that, after some initial amusement, even the soldiers were nauseated. Even the most generous of commentators cannot claim that the natives of the waterfront in Freetown harbour are of a high standard in looks or intelligence. I recall one of our soldiers leaning over the ship's rail next to me remarking, 'They all look like bloody missing links, don't they, sir? Especially that one with a Balaclava helmet on his head saying his sister hellish hot girl.'

The steamy heat of Freetown was the first experience of tropical weather for most of us, and the few who went ashore on duty for an hour or two said that we hadn't missed much and that they were glad to come back aboard.

The convoy sailed next day, far out into the Atlantic again; and as there was less danger from submarines, the troops were given some desultory training, mostly in the handling of weapons and lectures. However, the decks were so crowded that it was not very successful, especially since no one was accustomed yet to high temperatures day and night. We organized competitions and concerts of which I was appointed to be in charge. A boxing competition went well; and so did a crossing-the-line ceremony, during which, as senior officer, I had to volunteer to be lathered and scrubbed with a broom, and finally ducked in a canvas swimming bath, by Neptune's attendants, *pour encourager les autres*. We had some very good amateur artists aboard, and a sergeant who had been a stage producer; thus, in the middle of the Atlantic, we produced a splendid concert and revue, which ran for three nights so that all the passengers could attend. I recall that on this occasion I acted as compère and appeared before the curtain between turns, each time wearing a different costume, which were obtained from the ship's barber who had a stock which he let out for fancy dress dances in peacetime. Gunner Smith of my draft composed some original music, and one item, called 'Atlantic Rhythm', was played professionally after the war.

When we were well below the equator, our escorts relaxed a little, and the cruiser sailed up and down between the lines of ships to give us all the benefit of its marine band, which played lustily on the quarterdeck. We approached Cape Town directly from the west; and as our ship tied up at the quay, we were greeted by The Lady in White who was standing on the parapet singing 'Land of Hope and Glory'. This middle-aged lady became famous, known to tens of thousands of troops calling at the Cape, and it is said she never missed greeting a convoy in this manner.

The town itself was then a large colonial settlement with fine Victorian and Edwardian buildings, many built of timber, and it was a much more attractive place than the modern city. The troops were given a few hours shore leave, which was badly needed after seven weeks of a voyage which had still not ended. The inhabitants treated us royally, with profuse hospitality; and this was all the more generous of them, since a convoy containing Australian troops had recently done a great deal of damage there. The troops had been warned to be careful of strong drink, especially the Cape brandy, which is much more intoxicating than it seems at first taste. However the hospitality was too much for some of them, and there were some absentees when we sailed once more, this time into the Indian Ocean.

The tropical weather and the bad ventilation now became a sore trial, and the men began to suffer. There were several fatalities, fortunately not from our draft, due to sunstroke and also to actual suffocation below decks; and so we witnessed several sad funeral ceremonies of burials at sea, when the bodies, sewn in sailcloth and weighted with iron bars, are slid over the side by tilting the plank on which they are laid.

There were aboard three padres of different denominations, who performed these last rites. These three gentlemen of the cloth were foolishly placed at the same dining table, and they soon became belligerent, conducting a sort of triparte war, probably about their differing doxies. At one point during the voyage they had to be told that, despite their chaplains' appointments, they were still subject to military discipline and would be treated like any other offenders if they persisted in causing trouble aboard the ship!

The convoy sailed up the middle of the Indian Ocean, which was fortunately calm, and I was reminded of Kipling's line:

'There ain't a wave for miles and miles except the jiggle of the screw.'

When we neared India itself the weather became even hotter, but the officers still dined in drill tunics, wearing ties and collars. Before we changed into this rig we took sea-water baths; but soon we were again soaked in sweat with our tunics stained and crumpled, and eating became a burden. I doubt if any other army would have insisted that its officers keep up this standard of dress under those conditions, for during the hours of darkness all portholes were still kept closed, and the only ventilation was some hot air coming from louvres in the ceilings.

Nearing the entrance to the Red Sea the convoy split, some proceeding towards Suez, and only two or three ships turned for Bombay, where we anchored for a few days. A gunner officer on transport duties came aboard, and he invited me to go ashore and stay the week-end at the artillery barracks at Calabra, a splendid break in the long voyage. In the mess there I found myself in the atmosphere of nineteenth-century peacetime soldiering, and it seemed almost as though Kipling were still lurking about the place. During meals every officer had his own servant, dressed in splendid artillery livery, standing behind his chair, who relieved him of the fatigue of reaching out for cutlery and condiments. I was lent a splendid, almost grand, old, bearded veteran who looked as though he had followed Roberts to Kabul, and his assistant, a boot-boy, who fussed over me from morning to night, dressing and undressing me, and who would not be driven away. One of them slept across the doorway of my bedroom at night.

I also attended a tennis party, where I met 'the memsahibs', who showed little interest in the world conflict, except to hope that it would be over soon and that things would get back to normal. This was almost the last time that I saw the British Raj, with the sahibs and memsahibs in their full glory; and I will never forget the pomp and circumstance which existed in that small cantonment, and which has now departed. But even then things were changing: one of the first natives I met ashore was a small boy pedalling a 'stop me and buy one' ice-cream tricycle.

Our ship also called at Colombo, but we had no time to go ashore; and we sailed south again towards the Golden Chersonese, the lovely ancient name for the islands and lands about the Straits of Malacca. This was my first and unforgettable sight of the Far East; it thrilled me, and still does whenever I travel that way. South of Penang Island the views were enchanting, especially the little brilliant green islands with white lighthouses and bungalows nestling under palm trees, and the fishing pagars stretching out from the shores in the bright blue water.

When we were half-way down the straits, the officer commanding all troops abroad told me to prepare my draft for disembarkation at Singapore. Never shall I forget my first sight of the approaches to Keppel Harbour, as the ship sailed within a stone's throw of tropical islands such as I had dreamed of reading *The Orchid Hunters* as a boy; and I remember, too, the first peculiar sweet scent, or stink as some people call it, which makes one love it or hate it for life. As we moved nearer the quay, we heard the typical sound of Singapore in those days, the clack-clack of thousands of wooden sandals; and we saw sun reflected from snow-white buildings, and heard the leaves of near-by palm trees rustling in a slight breeze. We had been nearly thirteen weeks on our journey, and I thought the Lotus Lands well worth it.

The band of the Gordons played us in, to the tune of 'Great Little Army'; although we were neither great nor an army; and we felt embarrassed in our old-fashioned Wolseley pith helmets, and with our shorts hanging over our knees, for the troops on shore were dressed much more becomingly, with not one pith helmet amongst them.

Two officers of the garrison came aboard to greet our draft, Major Clarke and Captain Pearson, who were never known by these names, except officially, but as Changi and Fizzer. They accepted *stengahs* (whiskies and long sodas), and several more in quick succession; and then I learned from Fizzer that a new regiment of searchlights, part British and part Malay personnel, was to be formed. We thought that we might have been given this information sooner, so we could have learned the Malay language. No one seemed interested in what we had seen and done, coming as we did from the seat of war, nor in the Battle of Britain, all of which we were anxious to relate; and they departed until the next morning, when Changi appeared, wearing a lieutenant-colonel's insignia. He said, 'Good morning. I don't suppose you want me, Fizzer — see you all later,' and then he pushed off, and we did not see him again for several days.

A mountain of a man, RSM Pulford, appeared and took charge of disembarkation and transport to the cantonment of Changi at the eastern tip of Singapore Island. Here the men were lodged in sumptuous, airy barracks, so unlike those that we had left, that one gunner wrote home, 'Dear Mum. We are living in a palace.'

The officers' quarters, which had one of the finest views over the Straits of Johore and the China Sea, were magnificent; and mine, as a field officer, were almost ambassadorial. I had two immense rooms, each with a veranda, and an enormous, luxurious bathroom all to myself, plus the services of Ah Fong, a Chinese servant.

Our draft was divided into two to form two batteries, with Arthur Stiby commanding one and I the other. The NCOs were from a coast artillery regiment and had been given some instruction in the use of the lights before our arrival — some were excellent men, but others were obviously second rate and had been thankfully disposed of by their old unit. They were all regulars, and they showed a decided antipathy for men of the draft, whom they addressed as 'bloody conscripts' until we checked them.

We were all agog to learn what was to be our rôle in Malaya, but it was some time before we realized that our two batteries of searchlights were the only ones in the country. After several days of settling in, the new commanding officer called a conference, and we prepared to listen intently; but all we were told on this occasion was what social clubs we should join, and on whom we should leave calling cards as soon as possible. However, after a day or two, a staff officer gave us a briefing on the dispositions of troops throughout Malaya, a country about the size of the United Kingdom. Arthur and I listened with increasing astonishment as he swept his hand over an area on the map the size of Yorkshire, saying, 'Here we have a company of the Dogras.'

And then he indicated a stretch of coastline about ten miles long on the east coast, saying, 'Here we have a platoon of the volunteer force.'

There were some airfields under construction, and the anti-aircraft artillery consisted of three regiments, none with guns larger than 3.7 in. There were some heavy guns facing out to sea, all pointing the wrong way as it turned out, and a few regiments of British troops on the island. The total of fighting troops in the country consisted of two small Indian divisions, an understrength British one, and an Australian force, at that time of only brigade strength.

When the lecturer departed, Arthur and I remarked almost simultaneously, 'I hope to God nothing is going to happen here.'

There were very few in the country who were worrying, since most of the soldiers and civilians seemed to discount any idea of becoming involved in hostilities on land, and were relying on the Royal Navy, based at Singapore, to keep the sea lanes clear. Certainly the regular soldiers in our batteries felt that they would never have to go into action, unless they were posted to Europe or Africa. Many of them had been too long in the tropics—some for as much as seven years—and they were suffering from what is termed in the army the 'Deolali Tap',* which is supposed to make a man dull and forgetful, eccentric, with slight softening of the brain. For years they had not been given enough work—not their fault—and had become idle and apathetic, with poor morale. Before we arrived, their working day started early in the morning and ended at 11.30 hours, unless they were on guard; and most of them did 'charboy bashing' in the afternoons. Most of the fatigues, usually done by soldiers, were done by native servants; and so they were suffering from acute boredom, despite some sport and entertainment provided by the cantonment. It is difficult to shake troops out of apathy, since this feeds on itself, and so we decided to attempt it by some intensive training. In the beginning this caused a furore. It was too hot for outdoor parades in the afternoon, so I ordered a series of lectures on anti-aircraft defence during the Battle of Britain, the first to be delivered by myself. When I arrived at the lecture hall, I was astounded to see no regular soldier present except for the orderly sergeant. When I asked him why they were absent, he replied, 'Sir, this regiment never has parades after dinner, and we thought your order only applied to the new conscripts.'

I quickly disillusioned him and sent him to parade the rest of the battery, who appeared rubbing their eyes, surly, and highly disgruntled. It was a time for straight speaking, if not for actual disciplinary action, and so I said that although many of the draft had already seen active service and were quite competent, what worried me was the poor standard of NCO training and experience, and that I intended to improve this before we took up battle positions. The words 'battle positions' caused incredulity and some sniggers, and as I was very angry indeed, I added that if there was any further reluctance to parade in the afternoons, I would take the battery on the drill square and myself give it an hour's foot drill.

* Deolali was a holding camp in India where men waited for postings and troopships back to Blighty, with little to do for long periods under a torrid sun, which was supposed to make them unbalanced.

We had no further trouble, but long afterwards in 1947, at a reunion, I heard the sequel to this incident. One of those defaulters came up to me and said, 'When we got back to the barrack room we roared with laughter at you mentioning going into action—loathed your guts—but the lads did say "well, the TA bastard isn't wet and like a real fucking officer—we might do worse for an OC".'

I count this as the best commendation I received during my military service.

Within a few weeks of landing, we ourselves began to think that war was far away; there was no rationing and food was plentiful and luxurious, with whisky at 6/6d a bottle; and there was none of the sordidness of England under wartime conditions. At first, to we who were fresh from blackouts, bombings and casualty lists in the UK, the atmosphere was strange and discreditable, even decadent at times; and except that they were involved in the production of valuable rubber and tin, we thought that the European inhabitants should have been devoting more efforts to winning the war. However, to be fair, there were many men who had volunteered for service in Europe and were fighting there, and some who were held back in reserved occupations. But there was a lot of money about, and much money was being made by the people of the several races in Malaya; they were enjoying themselves in what was mistakenly called 'The Bastion of the East'. Morals change as one moves east, and Byron summed it up in the lines:

'What men call gallantry and gods adultery,
Is much more common where the climate's sultry.'

Within a week of my landing, I was being driven in a car by an officer of the garrison, when I found myself involved in a chase after his wife whom he had seen in another car with some man; and I was the embarrassed spectator of the row and recriminations which went on when the couple reached home.

People were very hospitable, and I have to acknowledge many kindnesses; however, the rank and file were not entertained much by the Europeans, although there were clubs run by voluntary workers. The best workers in this field were undoubtedly the Salvation Army, at that time commanded by the famous Colonel Harris, who also did magnificent work in Korea years later.

Unhappily, many soldiers visiting Singapore City finished up in brothels and contracted venereal diseases. A score of those from the garrison which was attached to my battery were under treatment when I took over. However one must be charitable; the soldiers had little social contact with European women, and Eastern girls are generally extremely attractive and devilishly nubile, especially those taxi dancers in the amusement parks which are a feature of Singapore.

A week after landing, Arthur and I were entertained at the famous Raffles Hotel by an officer of the garrison, where one of the guests was Tunku Makota, the Crown Prince of Johore. One of the ladies there remarked, to our amazement and horror, 'You have been a long time arriving, as we heard when you left England, and there are not as many of you as we expected.'

So much for security and secrecy—for Arthur and I had not known our destination until a day before landing. Japanese spies were quite unnecessary in Malaya, as nearly every man in the street could have supplied information about the strength of our forces and their dispositions to the Imperial Japanese Army.

We enjoyed ourselves famously for a few weeks as a relief from the journey, but many of the reinforcements were disgruntled from the beginning. Some were experts in their various arms and had seen active service, and expected that they would receive promotion and would instruct the garrison; but they were sadly disappointed. One case is typical. Travelling in our ship was a flight lieutenant, an expert in bomb disposal, for which he had been highly decorated. A few days after we landed, I met him wearing the badges of rank of pilot officer, and I asked him about this. He replied, 'I understood I had been sent here to instruct others with promotion to squadron leader, but the appointment has been filled by an officer of the garrison who has never seen a bomb and there was no vacancy for me in my rank, so I got an Irishman's rise in promotion.'

I quote this case as one of many; and I have always felt that it was because there were so many disgruntled and disappointed men in the army in Malaya that there was lack of enthusiasm and poor morale from the beginning.

The time came for us to take up what would be our battle positions. These were in the State of Johore, north of Singapore Island, and on the whole we were glad to do so, to feel that we should be manning them in case of hostilities. My company HQ were on a piece of waste land in Johore Bahru; the detachments were spread over a very wide area, in jungle clearings, rubber plantations, and one in the middle of several square miles of pineapple plants, and I now was able to make proper acquaintance with our Malay personnel.

The Malayan Peninsula contains people from diverse races, from primitive jungle folk, the Semang and Sakai, to highly cultivated westernized orientals, Chinese and Malay. Singapore Island contained more Chinese than Malays; but in the Malay States the bulk of the population were true Malays, although most tradesmen were Chinese or Indian. The true Malay, in any walk of life, is gentlemanly and polite, and usually careful not to hurt one's feelings; but, as they come from a race in which there was much tribal warfare and piracy, they can be very bloodthirsty indeed if their *amour propre* is affected. An expert anthropologist once remarked, quoting some lines from Byron: 'He is the mildest manner'd man/That ever scuttled ship or cut a throat.'

As Nature in that country is bountiful, two rice crops a year can be produced without much work, and the Malays believe in *dolce far niente*. Thus they are inclined to idleness and some introspection, especially if they are brooding on a real or fancied grievance; and too much of this can result in a man running amok, during which he will suddenly attack people, known or unknown to him, until he is killed himself. The Malays are fond of gambling, borrowing money, and they like fine clothes, so that the soldiers' uniforms were very attractive, especially the dress clothes which consisted of a purple *songkok* elliptical shaped fez with a sarong of silk in variegated colours. The soldiers were always impeccably turned out and better drilled than the British men. They were surprisingly efficient in using their searchlight equipment, but were poor shots with rifles or machine-guns. Their service dress was similar to that of Gurkha regiments, and indeed they looked like Gurkha soldiers wearing bush hats. I liked them, and I set about learning their language from the NCOs who spoke good English, many of whom had attended High Schools in the colony. If I did try to address them in their own tongue, they were delighted, and to spare my feelings they did not laugh at my mistakes but replied in simple words which they thought I could understand. In some ways they were like schoolboys, and often brought presents for their teacher. If a man was given leave to attend a wedding, he would return and ask to see me in the orderly room, where he would salute perfectly and then place on my table a decorated cup containing yellow rice and a coloured hard-boiled egg with a flower stuck in it. It reminded me of the 'paste egg day' of my childhood; my Malay sergeant-major explained that all wedding guests received such gifts, and that I was included because I had given the man leave. Since they were Moslems, we had to provide food different from that of the British troops; and the various fasting times, such as Ramadan, led to complications in administration.

We had men of other races with us, too, the drivers of the hired cars which were supplied by a civilian firm, since we were short of transport. One was a Sikh, one a Chinese, and the other an Indian, possibly a Madrassi; and whenever the subject of race relations is mentioned these days, I smile, for many people think that racial antipathy is confined to black and white. We gave them one bell tent for accommodation, and this was generous, for our British soldiers were eight to a tent. But the drivers could not get on together and bewailed their lot, complaining bitterly to the quartermaster sergeant who, of course, chased them away. Over a period of a few days after my arrival, each one in turn approached me privately, and each one using almost exactly the same words, pleaded, 'Oh, Tuan OC, please give me another sleeping place—I can no longer stay with these other drivers—they have coloured skins and are not of my race, and they stink —I think I may be murdered.'

I was particularly unsympathetic, thinking of the men who were eight to a tent, and remarked that there was a big war on, and that if they wished to have a private racial war they could get on with it—but that no extra tent would be forth-coming. Eventually the hostilities died down, when the drivers decided to sleep in their cars rather than altogether.

My own Malay driver became incensed when a dark Tamil touched my car; he got out, and before I could stop him, beat him up. When I ticked him off for such conduct, he simply said, 'I do not like black men.'

Solutions to racial discriminations are much more com-plicated than many well-meaning English people can imagine.

I commanded what was probably the most interesting searchlight battery in the war, and in the most curious sur-roundings; even before actual hostilities began there was always something odd happening. One night a rogue elephant emerged from the jungle near a site manned by British soldiers; he walked slowly across it, pushed over the heavy searchlight and, wrapping his trunk around the machine-gun, threw it into the bushes, as the sentry stood paralysed with fright. He said later that he felt less than the dust beneath its feet. Afterwards, a planter told us that we had placed the light precisely in the way of a faint path which the elephant used once every year to make a pilgrimage somewhere. On another occasion, a tiger, caught in the beams of a dispatch rider's headlights, streaked away in front of him for a mile or more down a jungle track. Occasionally, too, we were plagued by *hantas* (ghosts), for the Malays are very superstitious. There was one inexplicable incident: a Malay bombardier on a lonely site rang up and reported very officially that there was a ghost walking about the area among the equipment, and he asked, 'What orders, please, Tuan OC?'

I was nonplussed, never having had to make a decision concerning ghosts mixed up with logistics; but the bom-bardier seemed quite earnest and official. Fortunately, an old rubber planter, who was well acquainted with the customs and folklore of the country, took over the telephone and asked a few questions regarding the hantu. It appeared that it was a giant, fifteen feet high, with seaweedy hair and long fangs, and the planter decided that it was a well-known ghost called Si Gergusi (the Gummy One). The bombardier reported that he was not particularly frightened, but that his men were nervous; and although Si Gergusi was not interfering with his equipment, he would like to know, 'What orders, please?'

My planter friend replied, 'Bombardier, you wear a stripe on your sleeve and you know that something shaped like that is adequate protection from hantus, and your people put palm branches in this shape on roads to protect their villages, therefore your men have nothing to fear.'

The bombardier was quite satisfied, and when I visited that site the next day, an account of Si Gergusi's visit had been entered in the NCOs daily log — and no one except the Europeans found this strange.

Searchlights were much more efficient in the tropical darkness than in the misty atmosphere of Great Britain, where their value was often doubtful even though they used highly technical listening and radar apparatus. The Malay soldiers were better at detecting aircraft with their eyes and ears than were the British troops with their listening apparatus; and we were pleasantly surprised to find how easily we could pick up the sound of friendly aeroplanes, and when war came, of hostile ones.

It is difficult even now to understand the reluctance of so many people to believe that war was imminent, even when Japanese troops landed in Thailand preparatory to invading North Malaya. Social life, with many parties, picnics and clubbing, all of which included the consumption of much alcohol, continued frenetically; and dances took place at Raffles Hotel almost up to the time when the enemy entered Singapore. There were few air-raid precautions; and there was no proper blackout, but we had something called a 'brownout', which consisted of switching off some street lamps and the more glaring illuminations.

There were practically no field works constructed on Singapore Island itself, although there was plenty of native labour available. It has been said that there was no money available to pay workmen, and that if such work had been put in hand the mixed population of the country would have panicked. In my opinion, the Chinese, at least, who form the bulk of the population of the island, would have responded to a call to arms, since the Japanese were their sworn enemies. But there seemed to be no lead from the top civil or military authority, and so many individuals sank into lethargy and adopted the common Malay expression *tid' apa* (it doesn't matter) as their slogan.

Even the military training in most units was unrealistic. I remember a mobile exercise for anti-aircraft units, including my battery, which took place only a few weeks before hostilities, during which we proceeded up to the north of the State of Johore. It would have been almost comic if the situation had not been so serious: we were forbidden to do any damage to the country, which consisted of jungle and rubber plantations — we were not allowed to cut down trees for camouflage or to use certain roads, in order to preserve their surfaces. One night, at 02.00 hours, I was summoned to see the brigadier in command; and this incensed officer exclaimed, 'I learn that you have placed one of your searchlights and a machine-gun on a club cricket ground — what the blazes do you think you are doing?'

Surprised, I replied, 'Sir, the ground is the only open space for several miles around in which there is space to throw up a beam, as all the rest of the country is covered with trees and we are forbidden to make clearings. What must I do with the other lights to get them into action?'

I got no answer except, 'I have had the English club secretary to see me about using his field for military purposes — you will remove your equipment forthwith — I shall visit the site at first light to see you have done so and you will pay for any damage done.'

I went away to arrange the matter, marvelling; and I found that fortunately the troop commander had not placed his light and gun actually on the wicket, and that the only damage done was to the sides of a small gutter at the edge of the field. The brigadier did arrive as he had said, and together we solemnly inspected the almost unnoticeable damage.

By then I had received written orders for the next day's move, and somewhat diffidently I told him that I knew the road well since it was in my battery area. I said that it had numerous bridges over mangrove swamps and little creeks, which were posted as being fit for loads of only three tons. As many of my vehicles loaded were seven tons, I asked if perhaps he could permit us to use another route. He was astonished, since none of his staff had made a reconnaissance when they were preparing the exercise; and eventually the whole column had to be re-routed because the anti-aircraft guns could not proceed according to the planned moves.

It was this sort of attitude, which was displayed by many Europeans, and the *laissez-faire* feeling of many officers of all ranks, which worried many of us. We had seen action in Europe and the preparations in England to counter a German invasion made by soldiers, including the enthusiastic Home Guard; and we had known there the high morale of the civilian population. True, the climate of Malaya is inducive to physical and mental sloth; but British soldiers throughout history have fought under much worse conditions in the tropics, and I felt that troops of all ranks were living too soft, and that few commanders set out to train their men hard.

Although our battery was part of the garrison of Singapore and the personnel were counted as fortress troops with a static anti-aircraft rôle, as soon as we took up positions in the close-wooded country of Johore State, the officers realized that we might have to defend ourselves from ground attack as well as from the air, although this did not seem apparent to most of the rank and file. Our decision to brush up weapon training, in the use of rifles and machine-guns, was received with some incredulity by the gunners who were attached to us from the coast artillery regiment, mostly NCOs. They called rifles 'hand guns' and looked upon them with distaste. Only one or two of them were sufficiently knowledgeable to instruct the men, and most of them said that they had not fired a rifle for years. Since every combatant unit in the army is supposed to fire a musketry course once a year, I asked our RSM why they were so ignorant. He confessed at once that *he* had not fired a rifle for ten years; and when I enquired about the annual course he whispered that often the troops were not available for this training, but that the ammunition was fired at targets by one or two enthusiasts from the unit who were reasonable shots. Fortunately, all the men of my Woolwich draft had fired a course. However, most of the Malays had not, and when we eventually took them to a firing range the results were appalling.

When we were issued with some Mills grenades, few men had ever seen such before, and I, the battery commander, had to show NCOs how to prime them prior to use. I hoped that the Japanese, if they came, would be as casually trained as our own troops.

Shortly before the Japanese invaded Malaya, I received a telephone message from my commanding officer informing me that the GOC General Percival would inspect some of our sites the following day. I should remain at Battery HQ to receive him there after he had done so; and since he would arrive at about 17.00 hours, we should be prepared to offer him and his entourage some light refreshment. I asked what was the size of the party and got the reply, 'In addition to the great man himself, you may expect the fortress commander, two brigadiers, ack and quack types, an ADC, and, of course, myself; put on as good a show as you can.'

There was only myself and Captain John Kemp living at headquarters, in a bell tent, and with a small wooden hut which we called our mess. So while I attended to tidying up the camp, John, who was messing officer, rushed about the neighbourhood borrowing glasses, cups, and some chairs and tables. He also called at the nearest planters' club to obtain any liquor available, and gave explicit instructions to our Chinese cook-boy, Ah Fong, about making tea, cakes and sandwiches. The mess was transformed, and we were so pleased with our efforts that we hoped the general would not refuse an invitation to visit it.

Like the man in the front row at the Folies Bergères, he seemed very pleased with all he saw at headquarters; but he demurred at taking some refreshment, saying that the party was too large to entertain. His entourage was not so considerate, it had been a thirsty day for them; and our colonel, a thirsty man at any time, said he was keen to show how his officers made the best of things when roughing it away from cantonments.

So the whole party piled into our little *basha*, and John signalled to Ah Fong to brew up. I asked the GOC what refreshment he would like, mentioning that the kettle was boiling and that we had most drinks. He replied, 'No thank you, too much trouble for you officers.'

The rest of the party looked a bit glum, as they had had a wearing day, so I indicated that it would be no trouble since we had sufficient glasses, etc. and supplies. 'Well,' he said, 'perhaps I could enjoy a little fresh lime juice in a glass of water.'

I nodded to John, who turned white and shook his head. He was standing at the ice-box, prepared to serve almost every known spirit, beer, minerals and Coco-Cola, but he had not a single fresh lime. Nevertheless, being a willing officer, he signalled back that he would try to fulfil the order and left hurriedly by the window, as the doorway was crowded. To gain time, I asked everyone in turn what he would take, offering tea, whisky and beer; but all solemnly shook their heads and said they would take just a little fresh lime. Most of them were hard-bitten types and had not to my knowledge tasted lime, or even water, in years, but had downed *burra* pegs and *stengahs* during most of their service. All, that is, except our colonel, who whispered, 'For God's sake, man, give me a treble whisky, and speed up that lime as they are getting impatient.'

Ah Fong made matters worse by trying to give them cups of tea and cakes, which, to his astonishment, they all refused; and he stood baffled, almost with tears in his eyes. I heard one brigadier mutter, 'Pretty poor organization in this unit — the drink's a plaguey long time in coming.'

After what seemed an age, the GOC stood up saying, 'Glad

to have seen your little mess; I think we should leave now.'

At that moment John appeared at the window, sweating profusely after a speedy expedition to the local market; he sized up the situation and swiftly cut a lime in half, squeezing the juice into a glass. Ah Fong was on the ball and filled it with iced water and pushed it into the general's hand. He drank it, looking dazed, and left the mess without a word to poor John, who was sitting outside surrounded by fresh limes.

Our colonel dined out on that story for years with suitable comments. In some obscure way I have always associated this incident with the capitulation of Singapore.

Chapter 12

DOUBTS, DEFEAT AND
DISASTER

DURING the last few weeks of 1941, we learned of the attack
on Pearl Harbour, and that the Japanese had landed large
numbers of troops in Thailand. Owing to *force majeure*, that
country decided to join with the yellow men to form a
co-prosperity sphere of influence in the Far East. This meant
that the Thai army would join in any hostilities against the
British and Americans, or would at least remain benevolently
neutral. After a few weeks of Japanese occupation, the
majority of Thais loathed them, and they gave them very
little assistance in this unpopular war. (Few Thais ever did
fight against the Allies, and most of the Thai army spent the
war guarding frontiers in the north of their country.)

After these sudden belligerent actions of the Sons of
Nippon, one might have expected a stirring call to arms in
Singapore; but I cannot remember one, or even any particular sense of urgency. I think that many people expected that
the Royal Navy, based in the Straits of Johore, would deal
with any attempts to land enemy troops on the coasts of
Malaya, and that the huge fortress guns on Singapore would
destroy any force attacking the island itself.

Lieutenant Aspinal, one of our troop commanders, telephoning one day from a position overlooking the naval base,
reported that he had just seen the two great capital ships,
HMS *Repulse* and HMS *Prince of Wales*, setting sail in the
direction of the Gulf of Siam. A few days later I telephoned
him to give him the terrible news that they had both been
sunk by torpedoes fired at long range from Japanese aircraft.

When the news spread, the whole country fell silent; people talked in hushed voices and became apprehensive, and then alarmed, when they realized that the enemy had landed on the east coast of North Malaya.

Although later, as a prisoner of war, I heard a lot about the disasters suffered by our field force, the only first-hand account of the campaign that I can give is how it affected my little command.

Our battery was the first unit of the fortress troops to go into action when the enemy made their first bombing raid on Singapore at 04.30 hours on 8th December, 1941. We were on our positions in the State of Johore at readiness B, which was a condition of preparedness, but not an actual standing-to. Singapore City, which we could see from one of our positions, fifteen miles away, was only in a state of 'brown-out' and was clearly visible because of the many lights still burning — a splendid target. Captain Kemp, my second-in-command, was on duty in our little operations room, and I was half-asleep in my bunk. He received a telephone call from our most northerly searchlight site, which was manned by Malays: *'Kapal terbang ta' tahu'* — unknown aircraft — and immediately gave the order to expose the light and engage. When I emerged from my hut, three lights were steadily holding in their beams a flight of Japanese bombers. Other lights took over as they flew across our area and over the Straits of Johore, where they were then picked up by Major Stiby's battery. We waited enthusiastically and impatiently for the anti-aircraft guns to shoot or for our own aircraft to engage them; but nothing happened, except that we heard explosions of bombs in Singapore. Not until the enemy aircraft had flown back over our position, still illuminated, did a single gun fire, and by then they were out of range. We were astounded and grievously disappointed, as rarely during the war in Europe had we picked up such easy targets, which would have been shot down immediately being so brilliantly illuminated. This was the first of many disappointments, since we picked up every raiding force flying within range during our stay in Johore; but soon the Japanese flew too high for the 3.7 anti-aircraft guns to reach them.

From the opening of the campaign, there was never that spirit of determination which was so evident in Britain when invasion was expected; and most people spent their time discussing the day's disasters. In fact, some who should have known better talked too much, spreading alarm and despondency. The wife of a very senior officer in the garrison remarked to me within a few days of the landings in North Malaya, 'My husband says we will be unable to hang on to any of the peninsula.'

He was correct, but he should have kept his opinion to himself.

By the middle of December, the Japanese had advanced well down the peninsula and were not too many miles from our most northerly detachment sites; and it seemed that our forces could not hold them back. Odd units of the Indian division fell back or were withdrawn from action through our positions, and they appeared exhausted and dispirited. I became very worried at the prospect of pulling out of our positions, as many of the wives of our Malay soldiers lived in the villages which were about to be overrun, and they would have to be left there since the general policy was for the native population to remain static and not to flee to Singapore. It seemed a lot to ask of our native soldiers.

It was a dismal campaign, so the only bright incident in it is still fresh in my mind. It concerned our Christmas Waits. There were no tidings of great joy at Christmastide 1941, and the morale of both soldiers and civilians was low. Around our Battery HQ in Johore we had built up some machine-gun emplacements, dug some trenches, and had made as many preparations for its defence as possible under the circumstances — it was actually almost impossible to defend because of its siting, an attack on it had never been considered. We had also organized a mobile column manned by men from the headquarters, which would reconnoitre and deal with any terrorist attacks. It was similar to those we organized in the UK in preparation to receive German paratroops.

We were all feeling anxious, a feeling that I remembered before going over the top in the First World War; and I suddenly remembered the practice of my company commander there, Captain (now Colonel) Charlton, to prevent his men from brooding. He would walk along the trench a few minutes before action and start ticking off officers, NCOs and men, about long hair, dirty equipment, and suchlike — anything to distract their thoughts from the coming dangers. It occurred to me that the mobile column might visit the lonely sites and sing carols to cheer the personnel, so I summoned the BSM and told him to arrange the transport and to ask for volunteers. He went away shaking his head, but when he returned he said that every man had volunteered to go and was enthusiastically getting ready. As it was a bright night with little cloud, it seemed unlikely that we would be in action against Japanese aircraft, so I decided to go myself, leaving Captain Kemp and a few signallers at HQ.

Within twenty minutes the BSM reported all ready to move, and I inspected the column, probably the most highly armed bunch of carol singers which had ever taken to the roads. Every man carried his rifle and an extra bandolier of ammunition, two Lewis guns had been mounted on trucks, and my Malay driver had a wicked-looking kris stuck in his belt. A piano had been placed on a three-tonner, and one man had a guitar and another a trumpet. Our battery clerk was at the piano practising, and to my amusement some of the native servants had joined for service. There was little Amad, in a cut-down uniform, whom we had adopted as a battery mascot, as he seemed to be an orphan and had no home; there was Kitchie, a Chinese cook, who ran about shouting, 'Melly Clistmas'; and Mehru, our Tamil boot-boy, his face shining like the moon in a pool of tar, was sitting on the running-board of a truck, carrying his cleaning materials. The men were in great form, and the BSM remarked pithily to me, 'The only ruddy Christians I can see in this lot is coloured.'

The Battery Waits moved off, and we visited several detachments, who at first thought that the Japanese were almost on them; but they soon cheered up when we sang some carols and left them some beer. We ran into trouble when passing an encampment of Australian troops, most of whom were very drunk, and they threatened us with loaded rifles. There were no officers about, and it was difficult to explain that we were more-or-less peaceable carol singers; one, more drunk than the rest, put his head into the open window of my car and demanded to know, 'What this bastard Pommie major was doing.'

Our pianist sensibly started up 'Hark the Herald Angels Sing', and in a few minutes the diggers had joined in, with sentimental and alcoholic tears running down their faces. They demanded encores and clustered round the vehicles, and I regret to say that my car could proceed only after my batman, Berry, had driven his fist into the face of a digger at the window and knocked him on his back.

Our last call was at the bungalow of an English doctor, and we left our vehicles on the road and stepped silently up to the veranda. Gunner Berry, who had an excellent tenor voice, started to sing 'Silent Night', and the men joined in with feeling. The door of the bungalow opened, and the doctor appeared with his wife and two other ladies, all with hand-kerchiefs to their eyes. The doctor waited until we had finished singing, and then said with deep feeling, 'Thank you very sincerely, boys, we shall never forget this—come inside for drinks.'

He took me to one side and said gravely, 'We had all been feeling terribly distressed—the two lady guests are refugees from the north, and their husbands are missing—one of them had just remarked, "They will be singing carols tonight in England and we shall probably never see England again or hear carol singers", then your men started singing outside and I can tell you it seemed to us a sign and a visitation.'

The soldiers were in excellent spirits and did their best to cheer the ladies and to calm their fears. One, wiping her eyes said, 'Surely with men such as these we can stop the Japanese.'

But it was not to be—very few of those Christmas Waits returned to their homes, but lie in distant graves scattered over the Far East.

Our battery ate hearty Christmas dinners, with turkeys provided by well-wishers in the district; and for most of us it was our last decent meal for some years. Late in January I was ordered to move the battery back on to Singapore Island, as

only a thin rearguard of infantry and artillery was to be left
on the mainland of the peninsula; and during the move we
sustained our first casualties, in circumstances which are still
obscure. A heavy lorry with a British driver was sent by a
troop officer to pick up the personnel of a Malay detachment
in the middle of a large rubber plantation. It did not return,
so the officer went to discover the cause. He found the site
vacated and after some search found the lorry abandoned; the
British driver was dead at the wheel with a bullet through
his brain; but there were no Malay soldiers or rifles,
although the other equipment was intact. There were three
possible explanations: the first, that the driver had been shot
by a hidden fifth columnist, and that the Malays had fled; the
second, that the driver had been shot accidentally by the
bombardier who would have been sitting in the cab with a
loaded rifle; and the third, that the murder was deliberate,
as it was known that some native troops had been infiltrated
by enemy agents. I am inclined to believe the second explana-
tion, knowing the Malay mode of thought — they would
never have believed that they would escape punishment for
the accidental shooting. We had already had one native
soldier who had run (*'lari lari'* the Malay sergeant-major
called it) quite demented, because of a sharp reprimand for
some fault. Fortunately, he was caught before running
properly amok.

This incident was reported to higher command and
resulted in an order to place two British soldiers with each
native detachment, and eventually to remove Malays from
key positions.

On Singapore Island searchlights were now almost redun-
dant for an anti-aircraft rôle, as the enemy planes were
bombing at will. A 4.5 artillery AA battery had arrived from
England late in the campaign and had shot down a few of the
high-flying Japanese; but when they were hastily moved to
Java, the island was almost defenceless from air attack. All of
our few aircraft, which were obsolete from the beginning,
had been destroyed; and it had been sad to see these slow-
flying planes going off to their certain destruction. Day and
night the enemy bombers came over, flying out of range of

our 3.7 guns, and dropping their loads on any targets they selected. Most of our lights were posted for coast defence to point over the Straits of Johore, and I was horrified when I reconnoitred positions for them, for even then we had not realized how bad the situation was. On visiting the naval base, where we had to post lights and machine-guns, we discovered that the navy had gone, and that the floating dry-dock was sunk — scuttled. The personnel had left on such a sudden order that uneaten meals remained on the mess tables, and someone found a set of false teeth beside a plate. When I visited the boom defences to the east of the Straits, there was no guard or sentry; but I discovered a very senior naval officer in an office packing papers into a briefcase. He did not stop when I told him my orders, but simply said, 'You can do what the hell you like with the bloody place, I'm off,' and he went.

Battery HQ eventually established itself at the Singapore Racecourse, mainly because it was in telephone communication with most places. We had not yet seen a Japanese soldier closely, and we could not believe they could cross on to the island without a terrible bloody battle, since the causeway communicating with the mainland had been blown — but as it turned out, not thoroughly enough. We had two lights placed to illuminate it, and when I visited them a few days later, I saw a few of the yellow men walking about coolly on the mainland, and several of us could not resist having a few shots at them with a rifle although they were at extreme range. One or two bullets were returned by the enemy, without doing much harm, but we had slight satisfaction that we had exchanged fire.

There are a number of good and very adequate accounts of the final stages of the Malayan campaign, a very chaotic one once all troops had been withdrawn to the island of Singapore, but the following account of the activities and non-activities of my battery may give the reader a picture in detail of the confusion which was general. At Battery HQ we had most of the Malay soldiers and about sixty British; the remainder were manning lights scattered over most of the island, which once placed in position were difficult to move since we had only a few heavy lorries suitable for carrying the heavy equipment. They were not in telephone communication, but they could be visited by troop officers; however, if they were sited near other troops they were unpopular, since when the lights were exposed they drew enemy fire. Indeed, on one occasion men of a near-by Australian unit said that they would machine-gun and destroy a light if it was used.

Few proper defences had been built to face north across the Straits, although there must have been ample time and labour available to construct field works; breastworks could have been built, even though trenches may have been impracticable owing to water near the surface. Barbed wire was scarce, but entanglements could have been made from other materials — felled trees, etc. It is said that High Command was reluctant to prepare defences on the island itself, as this might create alarm amongst the native population, who thought that the war in Malaya could never reach Singapore. Although I am no military expert, it seems to me, with hindsight and experience on the Western Front in the First World War, that the position could have developed into static war; with the enemy sitting on the mainland, ourselves facing them on the island and with the Straits themselves as a 'No Man's Land'. True, it would have been difficult to man these defences with the remnants of the fighting troops; but there were tens of thousands of administrative troops, RASC, RAOC, and workshop personnel who could have been used, since their services were becoming quite unnecessary except to empty their stores, and eventually to destroy equipment. Within two days of the end of the campaign, my battery received sixteen brand-new searchlight mirrors, although we had been using practice reflectors which we had pleaded to have replaced six months before. The new ones had to be destroyed almost immediately and were never even tested. Our Malay soldiers had only three rifles among ten men, and they never received more; however, large quantities which had been in store were captured by the enemy, together with ammunition of all sorts.

There was a curious atmosphere of apprehension, even of despair, over the whole island, which now contained about

80,000 troops, mainly administrative and medical, sufficient for a large army; however, most combatant troops for the army had not yet arrived in the country. A fine division, the 18th, had just disembarked; and it was sent into action before the men were acclimatized and before their feet were hardened for marching, after months on board ship. It was never used as a division, but was split up into odd formations and used piecemeal, breaking the heart of its commander who died soon after the capitulation.

Petrol storage tanks on offshore islands and near the straits had been set on fire and covered the country with dirty smoke, which increased the feeling of despair. Military morale was not good, except in some outstanding units; I feel sure that the troops would have responded to calm, confident leadership, even to good oratory similar to that of Churchill. In my opinion, we were defeated even before the Japanese landed on the island itself; for the subsequent attack was a minor affair compared with even a small battle in the 1914 war. The shelling and bombardments were not heavy, and they caused comparatively few casualties; but positions were evacuated with little fighting and resistance.

The Japanese made their first assault on 8th February, across the Straits, and it succeeded in turning some of our units into a rabble; there were many deserters. Groups of one unit came through our position so hastily that we thought they were being pursued closely by the enemy, who in fact were still some miles away.

I received an order from General HQ stating that all units of whatever arm should form strong points with all-round defence. As we were out of touch with our commanding officer, I went to the AA brigadier at Fort Canning to ask where my battery should take up position to fall in with the general defensive area, since the racecourse was untenable, and in any case the stands were being used as a hospital. The brigadier sought out a senior staff officer and asked him where we should make a stand to conform with the general plans. The staff officer, harassed and tired, seemed to have no idea; and the brigadier, very incensed, remarked crisply, 'Well, you wrote the bloody order, who else can Peacock ask?'

I suggested that we might take up some position near the racecourse, and for want of any other ideas this was agreed; but the staff officer remarked, 'If the Japs get as far as the racecourse, it's all up with us.'

At the urgent request of a medical officer, we removed our men and a machine-gun from the tower of the stand, and spread the troops about in what we thought might be suitable firing positions. We soon had our first encounters with low-flying enemy planes, who were firing their machine-guns at any targets within range and dropping anti-personnel grenades. One plane suddenly swept over some trees close to where I was standing with another officer, near a sentry with a machine-gun mounted for anti-aircraft defence. We distinctly saw the pilot lean over the side of the plane and throw two small grenades directly at us. They exploded, making small cavities in the road, but miraculously no one was hit; we sprayed the craft with tracer bullets as it banked to fly away, and then it disappeared over the trees again.

I can still remember my thoughts and morale during the days before the end. Like everyone else, I was bone weary with physical effort, lack of sleep and poor food; and moreover I desperately wanted to bathe and remove some of the muck and sweat from my body. The Malay sergeant-major came to me too, pleading, not about being in action, but saying that the Malays had been unable to bathe themselves properly, and that this was a sore trial—they are scrupulous about cleanliness. I could only tell him his OC had not bathed either.

The climate of Singapore is very lowering, and after prolonged effort it is difficult to think clearly; I am sure some of my instructions may have been foolish. I cannot say that I was as frightened for my own safety as I had been in the battle of 21st March, 1918, although I had a strong foreboding that something was going to happen to me; but I found myself worrying about casualties and wondering, when a shell or bomb dropped, if the battery had suffered casualties. This was curious, since I remember that on the Western Front when shells dropped on a neighbouring position no one worried particularly, but were only thankful that they had not come our way. Such was the difference between the attitude of a young boy and that of a middle-aged man.

One odd incident occurred at the racecourse: a battalion of infantry appeared to line up for a counter-attack, and to my astonishment I found that they were Northumberland Fusiliers (9th Bn.), my old regiment; and that in command was an old acquaintance, Colonel Thomas, whom I had last met in 1929. I think we both said, 'Good God, what the blazes are you doing here?' before the attack went forward against a rather nebulous enemy.

We had to leave the racecourse after some sappers arrived and set fire to a store of thousands of motor tyres in the middle of our position—by this time all sorts of things, including guns, were being destroyed—and the smoke and pieces of burning rubber made the position intolerable, and attracted much shellfire. Then we received an order to turn ourselves into infantry, for which as an ex-infantryman I was heartily thankful; so now we could abandon our useless and cumbersome searchlights, concentrate all the men, and receive some definite orders. We managed to rest for an hour or two in a kampong, and most of us took the opportunity to have a wash and sluice. A sergeant, who had always been a troublesome NCO and had been court-martialled, was posted on guard with a few men; and when all the officers and most men were stripped to the skin, he suddenly panicked, shouting, 'Japanese tanks on us,' and fled.

There was great confusion; some men followed the sergeant, and a few were lost for a day or two; others returned after they had collected their thoughts. By the time the officers had hastily dressed, some army lorries came by, and it became obvious that it had been a false alarm.

Eventually we lay about the neighbourhood of Farrar Park in Singapore, in support of a very sketchy and shaky front line on the outskirts; Battery HQ occupied a private house, from which we went out on foraging parties for food, as the normal supply system had broken down. There was continuous light shelling and a great deal of spasmodic rifle fire all round; but the troop patrols whom we sent out to reconnoitre found the situation so confused, with bullets coming from all directions, that they could not tell who was firing at whom. Possibly some of the rifle fire was that of fifth columnists, shooting indiscriminately at anything in order to spread alarm. Large numbers of men, some obvious deserters and some quite lost, came through our position, and eventually we placed a cordon across a street and collected them; if we discovered that they had no official business, we held them and added them to our strength. Many were reluctant; however, one infantry sergeant, lost from his unit, shouted, 'I'll stay with these b——rs. They seem to know where they are, and they have some food.'

Shortly afterwards, an officer of the military police came to bail out from our posse two MPs, whom we had collected since they could give no account of what they were doing in the place and what was their duty.

The whole of Singapore City was in confusion, but it was not so badly damaged as many blitzed towns in England, for the Japanese bombs were not very large; but the roads were bestrewn with telephone wires, cables and poles, together with wrecked vehicles, broken glass and stones, through which military traffic picked its way in all directions. No one seemed to know the extent of the Japanese advance, and certainly the greatest majority of Allied soldiers never saw the enemy until the ceasefire. When we sent up troops of men from our battery to what was supposed to be the front line, we were shelled; but no one, including myself, saw any enemy infantry. I feel sure that most of the Japanese on the island at that time were imaginary, and that those present were in far smaller numbers than our own forces.

One of the last official communications I received at that time was a copy of a general order promulgated by General Wavell, the Supreme Commander in the Far East; and like most of the people who received it, I felt abashed and shamed, for rarely in the history of the British Army has such an instruction been necessary. It read:

'Special Order of the Day
It is certain that our troops in Singapore heavily outnumber any Japanese troops who have crossed the straits. We must

destroy them. Our whole fighting reputation is at stake and the honour of the British Empire. The Americans have held out in the Bataan Peninsula against far heavier odds, the Russians are turning back the picked strength of the Germans, the Chinese have held back the Japanese for four and a half years. It will be disgraceful if we yield our boasted fortress of Singapore to inferior enemy forces.'

General Percival had added this Special Order:

'In some units the troops have not shown the fighting spirit which is expected of men of the British Empire. It would be a lasting disgrace if we are defeated by an army of gangsters many times inferior in numbers to our own.'

During the night of 13th February, Farrar Park area was deliberately bombarded. I was awakened by a shell-burst about twenty yards in front of the house, then another shell-burst twenty yards behind, and I realized that this was what artillery men call a bracket, and that a third would fall between the two. Hastily shouting to the men to take cover in a slit trench dug in the garden, I reached for my pack, slung it over one shoulder, and came out of the front door just as the third shell arrived, with a scream and burst above and behind me, knocking me down dazed and concussed. I realized that I had been hit in several places; as I lay only partly conscious the BQMS and Berry, my batman, began to examine me for wounds, and one said, 'I think he's hit bad—get a car.'

Before I came properly to my senses to call for my second-in-command, I found myself being escorted by these soldiers to find a medical unit and realized that I was for the second time in my life *hors de combat*. It was difficult to find a medical unit which was receiving casualties, and we were turned away from several; but eventually I was carried into the cathedral and placed on a sort of altar, where my wounds were dressed, and where an Australian orderly, smelling strongly of drink, poured some rum down my throat, which did me little good and in fact nearly drowned me. We were turned out of the cathedral after a few minutes, and we eventually arrived at Victoria Hall, where my escorts, pushing

167

their way past an officer who wished to stop them, laid me down on the floor amongst hundreds of other troops and said farewell. The place was crammed with sick and wounded, some fit soldiers who were taking refuge, and some obvious deserters; it was like bedlam. A British army nursing sister (whom I learned later had refused to be evacuated with the others), seemed to be the only one there who was keeping her wits about her; I was distressed to hear her trying to calm men who had lost their nerve and were screaming at near-by explosions.

During the night I was bundled into an ambulance with other wounded, some seriously so, for one died on the short journey to Fullerton Building, a large office block being used as a hospital. During that trip I was more frightened than at any other time in my life, since the doors of the vehicle were locked and there were explosions all around us, and I felt that if we were struck we would not be able to escape. When the ambulance stopped I practically fell out of it and found myself lying half in a monsoon drain, so that when the others were carried into the building, I was forgotten. However, seeing a gleam of light around a blackout curtain covering a door, I crawled through it and up a flight of stairs and must have flaked out on a landing, as the next thing I knew was a voice saying, 'Here's someone bleeding—blimey, it's a bloody major.'

I was lifted gently and carried into a room full of wounded, where I was laid on the floor. Here I began to feel very ill, as well as knocked about, for I had caught dengue fever and was having rigors; I was unconscious when I was taken to an operating theatre. When I woke I found myself on a camp bed, and my first thoughts were about my pack and my boots —that both were missing. Half-delirious, I got out of bed, and crawled around the room, and found them in a corner intact. I am sure that this was an instinctive reaction, since previous experience had taught me never to be separated from my boots and kit. An elderly European lady, a VAD, got me back into bed; and when a stick of bombs straddled the building she held my tin hat over my head, until I insisted that she wear it. Strange to relate, I was sure now that I would not be hit again. As I mentioned previously, I had had a definite foreboding that I was going to 'cop it' in Singapore, and when I discovered that I was alive and only wounded, I felt certain that I would survive the war. This was an optimistic assessment for which I cannot account, since there was nothing in my present circumstances to support it: the pain from the wounds was trivial compared with the effects of dengue, sometimes called 'break bone fever'.

At that stage in the war the British were becoming accustomed to defeats, disasters, and evacuations, and I remembered the waggish Royal Navy commander of one of our escorting warships saying to me when we reached Singapore, 'I suppose we'll have to be back in a few weeks to take you off again.'

Lying in hospital, I could not help thinking of that other defeat on 21st March, 1918, and making comparisons with this one. Then, British soldiers had fought, sometimes hand-to-hand, against a numerically superior enemy, and when they were driven back, retired only a few yards at a time, suffering heavy casualties without undue confusion. In Malaya, retirements were of many miles at a time, mostly on wheels, and the battle casualties were few, although many men became lost and separated from their units. Later, an infantry officer who had been with the field force in North Malaya, told me that he never saw a Jap until after the retirement to Singapore Island, and only then after capitulation, adding that this must have been a common experience.

It seemed very possible that after the loss of the capital ships and all its air-cover Singapore would fall, but surely we could have held out much longer on the island, and could have sustained a true siege, which even if unsuccessful might have resulted in some glory. A longer defence might have saved Burma and shortened the war in the Far East. The official reasons for early surrender were: in order to save the lives of the civilian population; and because of the shortage of water, since the main reservoirs in Johore were in Japanese hands. Considering the daily torrential rain, the wells and the small catchment-areas on the island, it seems to me that the supply of water available would have sufficed for a few weeks.

There were good supplies of ammunition and stocks of food, and large numbers of soldiers, although many were not actual infantry. I have sometimes thought that if High Command had simply ordered every man who could carry a rifle or weapon to walk forward in the direction of the Straits of Johore, the enemy, astonished at the numbers, would have promptly retired to the mainland in confusion. We needed a commander like Henry the Fifth or the Iron Duke to rouse us with the proclamation, 'Up Guards, the whole line will advance,' but we had neither, and the campaign was a losing one from the beginning.

Perhaps the most apposite comment on the battle of Singapore is that made in a book written by a Japanese general, 'The defence lacked integrity,' and I do not quarrel with it. Being only a minor participant in the hostilities on Singapore Island I could not be fully aware of the overall situation; so my comments are mainly inspired by my previous experience in defence and defeat.

When I was wounded and made prisoner in the First World War, captivity was almost a relief after the horrors of the battle; but during my second spell as a prisoner of war, the captivity was much worse than the fighting. It was only luck which saved men's lives on the Western Front, and again only luck which enabled men to survive as captives of the Japanese.

Chapter 13

CAPTIVE ON THE KWAI

LATE next day an RAMC orderly rushed into our hospital room shouting, 'The Japanese are here.'

After a few minutes a most bizarre representative of the 'All-conquering Imperial Japanese Army' appeared in the room, a colonel, as we learned later. He was wearing pebble spectacles and one of our Wolseley pith helmets back-to-front, a filthy, dirty, sweaty cotton khaki uniform and crinkled top boots, which seemed to be killing him. He trailed behind him an enormous curved sword; he had not shaved for a week or two, and he seemed dead tired; he looked as though he had walked all the way from North Malaya through a mangrove swamp. He prowled around the room with his arms hanging down in front of him, making strange noises, which later we discovered was Japanese, and was followed about by an even scruffier soldier with a rifle. It took some effort not to laugh at him, after we had got over the first shock of seeing an enemy close to. We would have been terrified if we had known that just before the ceasefire Japanese soldiers had burst into another hospital, where they bayoneted surgeons as they operated, and had pushed patients out of bed and then shot them in the courtyard. An officer acquaintance told me some weeks later of his lucky escape. He had been told to get out of bed and go downstairs and was assisting another patient who was badly wounded in the leg. Their progress was slow, and half-way down the stairs an impatient, or friendly, Jap waved him back to his ward. Those patients just ahead of him were shot.

No one could communicate with our visitor, since he spoke no English and we were totally ignorant of his language. He departed as suddenly as he had arrived, and we saw no more Japanese for two or three weeks, during which my fever abated and my wounds were beginning to heal. Food and water were now very scarce, and I remember being given a drink which consisted of water with a little lime juice jelly stirred into it. There was no bread, only a few army biscuits.

The general feeling amongst staff and patients was of abysmal bewilderment that we should have capitulated to soldiers as curious and slovenly as the colonel and his attendant; but at the same time there was a sense of relief that they committed no atrocities and had left us alone in our temporary refuge, and that they had not molested the women.

From the accounts which I heard later from men of my battery of the entrance of the yellow men into Singapore City, they behaved reasonably at first, staring amazedly about them, as the barbarians may have done when they captured ancient Rome.

Much has been written about the tribulations of the prisoners taken by the Japanese army at Singapore, and in a book* published in 1966 I wrote a detailed account of the sufferings of my battery and of my own adventures during the next three and a half years, until the end of the war in the Far East. Limited space in this autobiography precludes me from writing another long account, but the following pages present the salient facts and my own observations regarding our long internment.

Immediately after the capitulation all the British and Australian prisoners were concentrated in the cantonment of Changi, situated on the eastern tip of Singapore Island. They were guarded mainly by renegade Indian sepoys who had elected to change sides. Other Indian soldiers and the Gurkha regiments remained entirely loyal to the British Raj, and they were interned in concentration camps which, ironically, had been built to accommodate captive Japanese. Within a few days, all the food that the white prisoners had been able to

* *Prisoner on the Kwai*, William Blackwood & Sons, to be obtained in most libraries.

172

carry to Changi had been used up, and they were reduced to a diet of rice, with trifling amounts of vegetables and morsels of dried fish. Even if they had wanted to, the Japanese could not have provided much better, once the stocks of British army rations in Singapore were finished. This unaccustomed diet was a sore trial to the soldiers. Some actually refused it, and weakened themselves from the beginning of their captivity. Everyone was abominably hungry and half-starved, and there was much sickness, especially the wasting disease of dysentery, and deaths were frequent.

I was taken to join my unit in Changi by truck, before I had recovered entirely from my fever and wounds, and so at first I did not feel as hungry as most of my companions. However, as I recovered I felt as famished as I did early in my internment in 1918, and I noticed again how hunger can sap morale and change the conduct of civilized men in their dealings with others.

The numerous prisoners were a great embarrassment to the Nips (as we called the Japanese), for they could not afford sufficient troops to guard against a revolt, since a large part of their army was sent on to conquer Burma soon after the capitulation of Singapore. Their command developed the ingenious plan of using the prisoners to build a strategic railway across Thailand to connect Bangkok and Moulmein to Burma, which would shorten their lines of communication by several thousand miles, cutting out the long sea trip around Malaya to Rangoon; and it would also ensure that the captives were isolated by hundreds of miles from any area of hostilities, making escape almost impossible. In order to carry out this plan, the Nips did not separate the officers from their men, but used our own unit formations as labour gangs until the railway was completed. They at first pretended that we were helping them in the development of the Far East; indeed, they adopted the principle that we had now changed sides, as was frequently the case in medieval warfare. Officers were made responsible for the conduct of their junior ranks, and they often suffered vicarious punishment for the misdeeds of their men. This is probably one of the reasons why, after we had been interned for a few weeks, there were few attempts to escape, since the senior officer would be blamed and would be in danger of severe, even capital, punishment.

During May 1942 I was detailed by British Command to take charge of a party of about two hundred and fifty officers and men, as a sort of leading prisoner; and we were dispatched, with hundreds of others, to Thailand by train. I would not like to repeat that journey. We were packed into small steel trucks in parties of thirty, where it was impossible for everyone to lie down at once. The journey occupied several days, until we detrained exhausted at Bahn Pong, where the railway construction was to begin. We were lodged in huts of bamboo and atap (palm leaf thatching) and were crowded, touching each other, on wooden sleeping platforms supporting one hundred bodies.

After a week or two, I was sent with my men up to the River Kwai to build the first camps for the reception of the thousands of prisoners coming from Singapore. The proposed railway track was to be constructed up the valley of this river, a place almost unknown to Europeans up until then; my party saw the country in its virgin state, and we bivouacked in the jungle until we made huts from materials supplied by the natives. Our food was a little better than in Changi: we had about ten ounces of rice a day, with vegetables and fried fish, and about one ounce of tea to thirty men. At times we could obtain eggs and pig oil from the natives, and without these many more would have died of starvation. Sometimes our rations were very sparse, and for two weeks we lived on rice, salt and tea. As their uniforms wore out, most of the men were reduced to wearing rags, and they worked almost naked, in loin cloths which we called Jap Happies. Boots wore out, and many were barefoot until the Japanese provided thin rubber and cloth boots for rough work on the railway.

After building a camp or two, we proceeded up river and were set to work building the railway itself. We worked almost with our bare hands, for our captors had few tools except picks and *chungols* (spade mattocks), plus some dynamite for blasting. One of our first tasks was to make a cutting through a rocky hill, and this was done with crowbars and heavy hammers boring holes (each one a day's work

174

for two men) to take blasting charges. After the blasting, the debris was carried away in little wickerwork baskets and was used for embankments leading to the cutting. Later, we made bridges and culverts, taking most of the timber from the surrounding jungle, and using a pile-driver operated by fifty men pulling on ropes. When one stretch of track was completed, we marched further up the river valley, leapfrogging through other parties, to start another.

As the men became weaker and more ill-nourished, there was more sickness and more deaths. The labour force suffered from almost every known tropical disease, and there were practically no medicines available to treat them once our own medical officers had expended those salvaged from Singapore. It is known that the Red Cross had offered to send food, clothing, and medical stores in neutral ships to Thailand for our use; but the Japanese were perverse and would not accept them, with the result that one-third of the prisoners on the Kwai died before the end. My battery was reduced by 40 per cent. The greatest scourge was cholera, which struck in 1943 and slew thousands within a few weeks. There was no remedy, except to drink gallons of water in which a few crystals of potassium permanganate had been dissolved. Cholera is a terrible disease which drains liquid from the body, reducing the sufferer within hours to a skeleton covered by skin. One of my party of soldiers contracted it at 1 o'clock at night and was dead and buried before midday the next day.

By the end of 1943, my party had reached Dha Kannon, a tiny settlement near the border of Burma and Thailand, about one hundred miles from our starting point; and there we met other groups of prisoners who had begun working from Moulmein. The rails were then joined, and the Kwai railway was completed as planned. It has been called the Railway of Death, and with some justification, since 12,500 European prisoners died during its construction; and uncounted thousands of native coolies, mostly Tamils, who were brought up from Malaya to assist in the work, perished of starvation and disease, since they had less stamina than we had and had lost their will to survive.

During the construction of this railway, even the most

unforgiving of prisoners recognized the skilled field engineering of the Japanese and their talent for improvisation. The project had been considered by the Thai government before the war but had been turned down as impracticable; it was the determination and perseverance of the Nipponese, plus their callous disregard for the lives of their labour force, which made it possible to complete the task in record time. The surveys and the direction of the work were done by a battalion of efficient railway engineers; but the administration consisted of poor types of Japanese officers and men, mostly Korean conscripts, since at the time Korea was a Japanese protectorate. Some of the guards were so moronic that they were easily duped, especially in counting the numbers of prisoners in their charge, having to rely on the word of the leading man.

The completed railroad was, however, of little use to our enemies, since it was immediately bombed by allied air forces, and few trains ever made the whole journey. During the later stages of the war, the prisoners too suffered from accidental bombing, and in one camp there were eighty casualties during one night. This camp, called Tamarkan, was situated near a large bridge built over the River Mehong and is the supposed location of the 'Bridge over the River Kwai' in the film of that name. The story is fictitious, but some of the shots in the film give a fair picture of the lives of the prisoners and of our working conditions.

By the middle of 1944, most of the working force had been withdrawn to base camps down river at Chunkai and Kanchanaburi, and the officers were separated from the other ranks. We were now much more closely confined, and I did not go outside the perimeter of Kanchanaburi for months. We were very crowded in my hut, which housed field officers and above (it was called 'The Imperial War Museum' by other prisoners). The sleeping space per man was only twenty inches wide and six feet long; just about the dimensions of a coffin.

During this period I took up dentistry again as a few instruments were found in the camp there, and I provided a sketchy dental service for both prisoners and guards. It was essential to treat the guards, whose gold crowns were always coming adrift, because they were the sole source of the necessary dental materials. We used to tell them that we had no 'cemento' or 'sleepo medicine' (anaesthetic), but that we would treat them if they would obtain these things from Bangkok. They had no Ha Isha (dentists) in their army, so they were pleased to have our services, and when they went on leave they always brought back the necessary medicaments. We used little of them in their treatments, but used the remainder for our own prisoner patients. The peculiar sort of dentistry that we practised on the Kwai has been described in professional magazines, to illustrate the value of ingenious improvisations.

Now that the main work on the railway was finished, our conditions of internment improved a little. More food was available, although it was still far below the standards sufficient to retain health and strength; and we organized games, and a concert party, since there was plenty of acting talent in the camp.

Although those three and a half years in Thailand were very hard and tragic, there were many amusing episodes which took place because of the widely different logic of the European captives and their oriental captors. I have often described it as a mixture of Grand Guignol, *Alice in Wonderland* and Gilbert's *Mikado*, because we lived with a background of death, misery and horror, but the unexpected usually happened in a topsy-turvy manner, and there were always the imponderable comic capers of our guards.

I remember vividly the deaths of three men of our battery, with even more sorrow than I do the others. On one occasion my party was helping sick men on their journey to a base camp and picked up a soldier who was just a living skeleton. We laid him down on the only space available on the ground in a filthy bivouac which had just been vacated by Tamil coolies. We did what we could to cheer him, saying the railway had now reached the camp and that he could now travel on it. 'No,' he whispered, 'I'm done for, mister—don't bother to carry me to the rails—I can die here just as well as in a railway wagon.'

He was almost too weak to sip from the mug of tea which

I tried to give him, supporting his back. Within half an hour he was dead, and we buried him in the jungle as soon as we could arrange a stretcher party. The last rites before filling in the grave consisted of a murmuring of the Lord's Prayer by the bearers.

One of our men died in a large camp well up river during the cholera epidemic, and an army chaplain was present at the funeral. It was a Sunday, a non-working day, so a score of the battery paraded as mourners. The sun shone hotly in the midst of beautiful scenery, which was scarred by the newly-made railway track. The padre, in a tattered surplice, led the way in front of the bearers, who carried the body, wrapped in straw sacks, on a stretcher of bamboo slats, while we mourners followed, stumbling over the railway sleepers, until we came to the funeral pyre of logs. At that time we had to burn our dead, and two senior NCOs collected wood and tended a continually burning fire. We laid the pathetic remains on the ground and stood with bare heads as the padre read the service and then turned about, leaving the NCOs to complete their grisly task. It is the custom after military funerals to play cheerful music, and I recall that we whistled 'Colonel Bogey' on the way back to camp.

Another of our soldiers who might have lived, died because of the criminal activities of certain bad men amongst us. He had been separated from my party, but we found him in another camp, desperately ill. He was so delighted to contact his comrades again, and to have some extra food that we obtained for him, that he started to recover. But one morning I found him relapsed and near to death. I tried to rouse and cheer him, saying how pleased we were at his improvement since we found him, but he murmured, 'No, I can stand no more—some men came into this hut last night and stole everything—they took my pack and I have nothing left—I'm finished.'

The poor man had nothing left in the world except half of a rice sack which covered his naked body, and, horrified, I said, 'We'll find you some kit somehow.'

But he died that morning of a broken heart, and I feel sure that if we had found the thieves, we would have lynched them.

As to the unexpected — a brother officer of mine was being bullied by a party of Nips in a sampan, in which a scruffy-looking Thai sat smoking. When the Japanese had desisted from bullying and departed, the Thai remarked in perfect, cultured English, 'Appalling manners these Japanese soldiers have. Now will you tell me if there are any OMs? (Old *Malvernians*).'

The surprised officer said, 'I'm one, and I know of five others.'

The Thai surreptitiously pushed several hundred ticals (the Thai money) into his hand, saying, 'Please distribute this among them; you see, I am an OM too.'

He was no doubt a spy from the Free Thai Army, a resistance force which was being organized. I also chuckle at the pun which someone made about this incident: 'Evidently a *Thai* of the Old School.'

On another occasion some of us were buying eggs and bananas from some peasants, when our crazy Japanese sergeant (Yotanne Gunso) appeared, very wrathful; we expected a few blows, as trading was forbidden, but to our surprise he beat up the traders for overcharging us. Physical punishment is usual in the Japanese army, and our guards could never quite understand why we objected to it.

The perversity and sometimes inexplicable reactions of our guards were a great trial, since we could rarely foresee the outcome of some incident. Trivial misdemeanours could end in severe beatings and in tragedy, and grave offences might be shrugged off, as happened once in my party. One of my soldiers accidently killed a Thai peasant, and several of us, including me, the leader, expected to suffer terrible punishment; but after confused investigations by the military police, the soldier was lightly punished for *speaking* to a Thai, not for *killing* him. I had one or two spells of standing in front of the guard hut for omitting to salute a sentry, and one ended in high comedy when a Japanese sergeant slipped on a banana skin and fell on his back while he was trying to kick me.

It was possible to trick some of the silly sentries when one was a leading prisoner. British officers who were supposedly supervising the work of other prisoners tried to prevent beatings being delivered for no obvious reason, and on several occasions we successfully managed to use the following subterfuge. As the beating was about to begin, or had begun, the officer would interpose himself between prisoner and sentry and pretend to be very angry with the worker, shouting at him, 'Don't take any notice of what I am saying but stand to attention and look frightened.'

He would then himself threaten the prisoner with a stick, screaming abuse. The prisoner, playing his part, would cringe and then stand to attention, expressing contrition for his fancied misdeed. The sentry would look on with approval at the fancied disciplining, and the prisoner would be let off. On one occasion when I used this trick, the sentry patted me warmly on the shoulder, saying, '*Kujacku Shosa velly good sodger number one shoko.*' (Major Peacock a very good soldier and first-class officer.)

As the war drew to its close, there was much Allied air activity, especially bombing and reconnaissance missions. The more approachable Korean guards referred to the latter as 'Come look see go back speakie planes', and became very excited at the approach of hostilities in Thailand. About three weeks before the end, I was moved with one hundred other officer prisoners to a distant camp west of Bangkok. We had a terrible journey by train on top of trucks, then in crowded sampans, ending with a march of forty-eight kilometres, in a temperature of ninety-five degrees. We were in the charge of a sadistic Nip sergeant-major who was determined to create a record in troop movement, so that march was the most arduous of all my military service, and we reached our destination, Nakom Nai Yok, dead-beat. After three weeks in that camp, which had about it a brooding atmosphere of pending calamity, the war came suddenly to an end. The Japanese simply moved out, leaving us to look after ourselves, assisted by the local Thai authorities who sent us meat on the hoof. Allied planes flew over and dropped clothing, food and cigarettes; and eventually we heard of the delivery of the atom bomb, the destruction of Hiroshima, and the Emperor's order to his armies to lay down their arms.

There is little doubt that the use of the bomb saved our lives. Most of us who were prisoners in the Far East firmly believe that if the Emperor had not ordered a capitulation the Japanese soldiers would have fought on until they were decimated; and in doing so that they would have massacred their captives who would only have been encumbrances. I agree with the many knowledgeable military experts who consider that the Japanese are some of the toughest and bravest soldiers in the world, most of them fearing dishonour more than death. Very few of them were ever made prisoner; it was for this reason that our captors could not understand why we surrendered in such large numbers, instead of seeking honourable deaths in battle, and that is why they treated us (especially the officers) with disdain.

It was a fortnight or more before we left Nakom Nai Yok and were transported in Japanese trucks to Bangkok airport, from where we were flown in batches to Rangoon. The RAF discovered that my son, Gerald, whom I had last seen as a schoolboy, was serving as a navigator in a special squadron, which was based in India for operations over Japan; and he was flown to meet me in Rangoon. We had not met for four years and so our mutual delight and happiness can only be imagined. I learned from him that my wife, Penny, after service in the WRNS was now a Red Cross nurse and had volunteered for work in the Far East hoping to find me since I had been missing for years, but she had not left England; so we were able to communicate by letter and telegram.

I sailed home in comfort with hundreds of other ex-prisoners including one or two of my original draft from Woolwich, in the SS *Orbita*. As we neared the docks at Liverpool the ship's captain remarked to me, 'When you came aboard you all had a queer staring look in your eyes, and I expected trouble, but you are still better disciplined than most troops, and I have been delighted to carry you home.' Curiously, other persons, including nurses, remarked that the prisoners differed from the other troops, and Gerald said he could recognize that they were mainly pre-war regular and Territorial soldiers.

Penny and I met on the gangway after the ship made fast,

but at first we could find little to say to each other in our happiness. Next day the relatively healthy ex-prisoners were documented and given a brief medical examination, and we were then dispatched to our homes. Penny went on ahead to prepare the flat which she had rented after our house had suffered bomb damage; the flat too suffered from the effects of a V2 rocket. I was delivered there in a St John's ambulance, and I recall with a wry smile that the driver and his mate sat for over an hour in our lounge drinking tea, not thinking that Penny and I wished to be alone together. We have rarely been separated since.

Next day Sergeant Wiseman, one of my original unit formed at Hackbridge, called to see me, having just heard the news I had returned home and invited me to attend a reunion of 327 Company which he had arranged. When it took place I learned that I had been reported killed in Malaya, and Major Surridge who had taken over command from me read out the news on parade and ordered 'present arms'. I felt honoured but also amused, because few people receive news about their obsequies, and remembered the words of Mark Twain when he read in a newspaper that he had died, 'The report of my death was an exaggeration.'

ENGLAND, HOME
AND ABROAD
AGAIN

Chapter 14

ENGLAND, HOME AND ABROAD AGAIN

I WAS reasonably fit, having put on two stone in weight since release due to rest and good food during the voyage home. All prisoners were emaciated during captivity and in 1945 I was down to six-and-a-half stone, but fortunately had escaped dysentery and malaria so was not an invalid. However a candid friend at first sight of me at home said I looked like a scrawny chicken on a slab.

After the first excitement and rejoicings of repatriation had subsided I travelled to Newcastle to meet the rest of our family, and experienced that sensation which I have to this day when descending from a train at the Central Station, 'This is my own, my native land'. It seemed little changed and I think the same ticket collector who had taken my tickets during the First World War was still in his little box at the gate of the main line platform.

I stated in the first chapter of this book that people in the North have long memories, and it is a peculiar fact that I rarely emerge from the station without being greeted by some old acquaintance using my Christian name who will tell me what I have been doing since our last meeting. Sure enough an old schoolmate was waiting about in the central hall, stopped me, and remarked, 'What fettle, Basil? — we haven't been seeing ye for a few months — aa heor ye've been catched by the Japs — are ye aal reet noo? — when are ye gannin back?' (The Geordies never ask how long is your visit but when are you leaving again.)

During my internment both my parents had died full of

years and I learned that my father, poetical to the last, quoted Rabelais just before closing his eyes for the last time: 'Draw the curtain, the play is ended'. My sisters were still living in their house in Fenham. Uncle Archie was still alive but feeling his age. He had managed to get a paid job in Civil Defence by suppressing the fact of his enlistment in the army in 1879. His wife, Aunt Louie, told me that he had said 'I shall keep alive till Basil comes home.' I was able to see and chat to him but he was very weak and only a few weeks later I attended his funeral. Afterwards, when I escorted my aunt back to her home, she handed me his medals and original 17th Lancer tunic buttons showing the regimental emblem, a skull and crossbones, saying, 'I know that your uncle would like you to have these.'

It was March 1946 before I was summoned to appear at Guildford for release from the army almost eight years since I put on uniform for the first mobilization of my regiment. Seeing my army number 2142, the officer in charge said, 'You must have been given that a long time ago so you will be pleased to have a complete discharge.' I was not too gratified as this would have meant good-bye to part-time soldiering. Also, when I pointed out that I was due to receive a second bar to the Territorial decoration within a few weeks and the correct word for TA personnel should be 'disembodied' he posted me to the TA Reserve. Later, on the re-formation of the Territorial Army I found I was too old to be re-employed on the active list.

I was pleasantly occupied for a few years in a large general hospital practising as a dental specialist amongst congenial medical colleagues but I found life a little dull after the excitement of previous activities and rationing of nearly everything in Britain was an irritation. When I got the opportunity of visiting the Far East again I jumped at the chance. During 1950 the government asked for volunteers from the National Health Service to undertake medical and dental work in underdeveloped countries, offering secondment to them for three years after which the volunteers could return to their original posts. Penny was anxious to see the wonders of the

Far East so I applied for a secondment to North Borneo, then a colony, and received the posting mainly because I could speak a little Malay, the *lingua franca* of the region. I doubt if there were any other applicants. I had wanted to see Borneo since a boy when I first read *The Orchid Hunters*, so I got my wish. As my old batman had said, 'Once you have been in the jungle—the jungle will call you back.'

During our preparations for departure to the other side of the world I remembered that as a Reserve officer I should inform the War Office about my change of address. A few days later, when I was at the hospital, Penny received a telephone call from some department asking for me to call back immediately I was available. When I returned home Penny said, 'They are after you again—I hope you are not going to be called up for the fourth time since we were married.' I called a special number at the War Office and was asked to give details about my movements and informed that I might receive further instructions at Singapore. I never did, but learned years later that volunteer forces in the Far East were then being re-formed in preparation for a scratch force being sent to Hong Kong as there was some possibility of a confrontation with Red China.

Our voyage to Singapore was a delight for we travelled in luxury so different from my first voyage there in a troopship. When our ship, the *Canton* of the P and O Line, made fast at its berth I saw no signs of the late war, but there on the quay was a Malay soldier in uniform waving to us as we leant over the rail. He came up the gangway and I recognized him as RSM Jamin bin Marsam whom we had last seen six years before when he had attended the Victory Parade with a few others of the regiment. We had entertained them in our home and I remembered I had remarked casually, 'I must return to Malaya some day,' not thinking I would ever have the opportunity. I had dropped him a line after my appointment just stating I was going to Borneo. Jamin saluted and I asked how he had discovered we were on this ship. '*Khabar angin Tuan*,' he replied (news upon the wind), and we were in for another surprise when he continued, 'I have assembled every Malay soldier who knew you in the past and they are waiting for your inspection at the barracks.' Naturally Penny and I scrapped all plans for touring the city and accompanied him to the offshore island of Blakang Mati, his military station. Two score Malay soldiers were waiting in the canteen and the RSM called them to attention adding, *'Tuan OC, orang tua sudah balek.'* (OC, sir—the old man has returned.) I stammered a few words part Malay and part English to thank them all for this unexpected and kind welcome, then called for drinks all round. After half an hour reminiscing with individual soldiers, some of them now pensioners, Jamin took us off to his quarters to take a stupendous curry tiffin served by his pretty wife. She, to Penny's astonishment, disappeared from the dining-room and was discovered squatting on the floor in the kitchen eating her meal with her fingers in true Malay fashion. No one had heard of Women's Lib twenty years ago in the Far East.

After Penny and I had said farewell to our friends, and later were sitting in the lounge of the Adelphi Hotel in Singapore two Englishmen who had been sitting at a near-by table greeted us, and I recognized them as ex-POWs who had been with my party on the Kwai. They were educated men, one a schoolmaster, the other a colonial civil servant who had been in the ranks of the Singapore volunteers before and during the Japanese war. We joined them for dinner during which one reminded me, roaring with laughter, that during one of the most horrendous days on the Kwai I had reproved him for some triviality by saying gravely, 'I do not think you are a very good soldier.' Later sweating under a mosquito net again I thought what a wonderful day I had had on my first return to the Far East.

During our journey to North Borneo on a small coasting steamer we called at the island of Labuan. We went ashore there and came across a newly completed war cemetery where to my surprise and sadness I saw the graves of fifteen British soldiers who had served in my battery in Malaya. These men, taken prisoner at the capitulation, had been despatched early in captivity by the Japanese to an unknown destination. Some of them had been simple souls from the mill towns of

Lancashire and I feel that most of them had no idea where in the world they had been transported to.

Next day Penny and I landed at Jesselton, capital of North Borneo, known as Kota Kinabalu in Sabah, East Malaysia after Malaya gained its independence. Our experiences in that land where I was the only dental surgeon in an area the size of Ireland have been fully described in two previous books of mine *Peacock's Tales*, privately printed, and *Discursive Dentist* published by Heinemann.

This present book consists mainly of military memoirs so I feel our adventures in bringing some modern dental care to some native people who had not known what they were missing would be out of place in it. However, during my tour of duty in Borneo I occasionally found myself wearing a uniform again. Within a few days of arrival I was pressed into taking command of a small St John's Ambulance Brigade, numbering about thirty which turned out on ceremonial occasions and paraded behind the detachment of armed constabulary. Though this far-off land was still mainly primitive with few of the amenities of developed countries I thoroughly enjoyed the three years I spent there. North Borneo has been called 'The Stealer of Hearts' and it certainly stole mine. When leaving it—as we came—in a small coasting steamer, beginning our journey back to England, I gazed at its haunted mountain 'Kinabalu' thinking sorrowfully that I would never see it again; but I was mistaken.

ROADS BACK

Chapter 15

SLOW BOAT TO THE ORIENT

WITHIN a few weeks of our arrival in England I took up my duties again as dental specialist in my old hospital and time passed so quickly that I was astonished and a little shocked to receive a brief communication from the SW Metropolitan Hospital Board, informing me that on my next birthday I would be retired having reached the age for superannuation. Though I felt I was by no means 'burnt out'—an expression used on old military discharge papers—and possibly could have continued practising my profession for a few more years I decided to 'stand not upon the order of my going' but go at once, when still fit enough to enjoy life.

I was entitled to a modest pension which with care would keep my wife and myself in reasonable comfort, and a few hundred pounds gratuity. This was not enough to invest so Penny and I decided to blue it on another trip to the Far East to see it once again before modernity had spoiled its charm. Within a few days of my retirement we sailed on a Dutch cargo ship the *Neder Eems* bound for twenty ports in the Near and Far East. The duration of the voyage was five months and the fare if we had travelled in a liner would have been astronomic, but we paid only a few hundred pounds for the most enjoyable cruise we have ever made. The ship carried a maximum of twelve passengers but most of them disembarked en route, and for periods Penny and I, making the round trip were the only ones aboard. The ship's officers were attentive and our travelling companions congenial so our holiday was without blemish.

We became very friendly with a frail-looking Dutch RC priest who was returning to his very isolated parish in Luzon in the Philippines. He said he expected to die there as priests of his faith were rarely relieved of their duties. His name was Father John and he entertained us with many anecdotes about his life in the orient. Like many Dutch priests he was a bit of a rebel against the high authority in the Vatican. Two of his complaints being that he was forced to be celibate and had to wear clothes in the fashion of the thirteenth century. On board ship he always wore a T-shirt and shorts, and only put on his clerical dress when he went ashore in large towns where he had to meet others of his cloth. He had a wry sense of humour and when we were lying off Djedda, the pilgrims' port for Mecca, he bemoaned the fact that he could not get ashore to make the pilgrimage and become a Hadji. 'Just think,' he said, 'if I could get a double qualification as both RC priest and a Hadji in the Moslem faith, what I could do for the heathen.' When the Germans invaded Holland he was studying at a seminary. His sister hid him behind a large window pelmet when his home was searched, so that he would not be taken to do forced labour in Germany. He was living on the road used by Allied troops when fighting their way to the Rhine, and amused us with his observations about them. 'When the Americans or Canadians came through our village we locked up all our girls, when the Australians came we locked up all our silver, when the Scotsmen came we shut all our doors and windows to keep out the noise of their swearing and bagpipes. If the English came through they pestered us for hot water for shaving and making tea. One day a convoy of British tanks halted in the street and immediately the men jumped down and started shaving using mirrors propped up on the sides of the vehicles. I knew that there were still many armed enemy in the neighbourhood and as I could speak good English I mentioned this to a sergeant. He replied still lathering his face, "Right, sonny, when we have had a wash and a cup of tea we'll attend to the buggers." ' Father John commented on this incident, 'I had studied English history and read about Drake playing bowls when the Armada was approaching and saying there was time to finish the game and thrash the Dons too, but I never understood the story till then.'

The *Neder Eems* called at Singapore and once again we wandered about in that humid city, and had time to visit Johore Bahru to see the site of our old Battery HQ; now it was covered with a new housing estate, but in a wood close by we found the remains of one of our old company cars which I remembered had been hit by pieces of a bomb twenty-one years before. The house in Farrar Park in front of which I had been wounded still showed signs of shell damage, and the building which had been used as a temporary hospital was now a busy commercial office.

Our ship's itinerary was unexpectedly changed and to our delight we called at Jesselton and other ports in North Borneo where we received wonderful kindly greetings from old friends of several races, and a lavish dinner given by the Chinese tooth smiths (unqualified dentists). As we were leaving these good people again, with great regret, my old dental assistant Mr Tam remarked, 'When the white men leave Borneo they all say they will return, but jigger me Dr Peacock and his missus are the only ones who have done so.'

After calling at Manila, the most distant port in the voyage, the *Neder Eems* turned about and sailed for the Gulf of Siam and Bangkok. By an extraordinary trick of fate our ship moored at a wharf exactly opposite the large godown (dockside shed), in which I had been incarcerated with other POWs nearly twenty years before. Luckily there was a great deal of cargo to be handled so that we had five days in which to explore the city. There was time also to make a fantastic visit to the River Kwai, so Penny was able to see where her husband had been spending his time when missing for several years. We travelled in an air-conditioned hired car, the price for which was reduced for an ex-prisoner because, the manager said, 'You work on railway—not dead yet—you must have iron bones.' At Kanchanaburi, eighty miles from Bangkok I hired a dug-out canoe with an outboard motor and chugged a few miles up the Kwai to the site of the first camp my battery had built preparatory to starting on the railway construction. A few native houses had been built there replacing those we had destroyed in 1942, but most of the area was now a large military cemetery, made and maintained by the War Graves Commission. Many headstones bore the names of soldiers with whom I had served. It was sad to think of them lying there so far from their homes, but their graves were now in a beautifully tended garden under fragrant frangipani trees instead of rough jungle. The scenery round about was beautiful, though I doubt if any of us appreciated it during captivity.

Returning to Kanchanaburi, a hot untidy town, much the same as I remembered it, I noticed a house built in Chinese style with giants painted on its double doors. It reminded me, with a chuckle, how I had sat on the steps holding the rifle of my Japanese guard while he was having his pleasure inside with a 'comfort girl', and his extreme disappointment at her entertainment. A rather humourless Scottish officer was with me at the time who remarked, 'We have now reached the depths of degradation—two British officers sitting outside a brothel waiting on the pleasure of a barbarian.' Near by, too, was the dirty dram shop where on Christmas Day 1942 I had been left by a crazy Japanese sergeant and allowed to buy and be given bottles of Thai hooch from the owner and customers. Penny was becoming distressed in the intense heat and even I was surprised we had been able to work in it for three years, so we returned to the ship. As my wife slowly climbed the gangway she remarked, 'You must have had a guardian angel,' and I felt inclined to agree with her.

Bangkok is a remarkable city renowned for its many exotically beautiful temples and shrines among which we wandered for hours, admiring the work of the builders and delighted by the courtesy of the worshippers and the yellow-robed priests. In one, we paid a few pence to have our fortunes told by the Wheel of Life—something like a round table top with a rotating arrow in the centre. When this arrow was spun it stopped at a number which had to be told to a waiting priest. Our priest looked exactly like the well-known actor Alastair Sim; when I told him my number 17 he searched through a box of bamboo tubes, produced one, and removed a piece of paper rolled up inside it. Our guide translated the Thai writing as follows, 'You are just like the hunter who walks in the jungle and gets thorns in him. So try to bear up to these things and you will get what you want. Concerning luck you will always get what you want but will meet trouble on the way — you must always try hard. If you have a mistress — it is good for you.' Penny said she thought it all appropriate except the last line. Penny's number unfortunately was missing in the box of tubes. The priest chuckled, looking more and more like Alastair Sim, and said, 'Poor lady — no fortune for her.' He offered her another go on the wheel but she declined saying he could have her fee as a subscription to his temple.

Our voyage back to England was delightful but uneventful, but within a few minutes after entering our house I received an urgent message from the St Helier hospital secretary asking me to return to work for a few months as *locum tenens*. This recouped some of the expenses on our cruise and led to my taking up practice again many times during the next few years until I found it difficult to operate because of pain and disability in my right shoulder. My hospital colleagues gave me sympathetic treatment, and eventually referred me to the Ministry of Pensions suspecting that the disability was due to gunshot injuries received at Singapore. A medical officer in the Ministry, discovering from my army records that I had been a prisoner of war twice and on the River Kwai, insisted that I should be admitted to a military hospital for full investigations. A medical board, the members of which seemed surprised I had not been boarded years before, then awarded me a disability pension, having decided that my complaint was due to injuries at Singapore which had never been properly treated.

I felt a little abashed till an old army friend remarked, 'But any soldier is entitled to a bit of baksheesh on occasion if the sergeant-major is not looking.'

Although unfit to practise my profession, fortunately I had time to write stories and articles for magazines and also to study military history. Once again I became closely associated with my infantry regiment, The Royal Northumberland Fusiliers, and was very pleased to be selected to write its history which was published in the Famous Regiments series produced by the publishers of this present volume.

Chapter 16

LES COMBATANTS ANCIENS

During September 1965 my brother Jim and I decided to revisit the battlefields of the Western Front; we were prompted to do so by a casual remark that it was fifty years since he had first landed in France, on his way to the front in the ranks of his first regiment, The Royal Fusiliers.

We met on number fourteen platform at Victoria Station, the actual platform from which very many thousands of soldiers had entrained more than half a century ago *en route* for Dover, Folkestone and the Channel ferries. We were dressed in rough clothes and were travelling light as we expected to do much walking, so I was equipped with an old army pack which I had carried in the last war. Both of us were in great form and as we settled ourselves in our booked seats and summoned a waiter for coffee, Jim remarked cheerfully, 'Ah this is better than ten men with all their kit and rifles in one compartment,' and I added, 'Yes, and two of them drunk.'

We were a little disappointed that the paddle steamer *Brighton Belle* was no longer in service, as we wished our journey to be as similar as possible to those in the old days, albeit with more comfort. A smart British Rail boat took us across the Channel on an even keel, so we were able to eat a splendid lunch washed down with rather more drinks than we are normally accustomed to take in the middle of the day. We sat in comfort at a well-laid table and agreed that this was preferable to squatting on the deck gnawing haversack rations and being sea-sick.

Calais failed to stir old memories as the old buildings had disappeared, destroyed in the Second World War, and the new ones looked as though they had been built with breeze blocks. So within a few minutes of landing we took a train destined for Lens. Soon the names on the stations *en route* brought back a little nostalgia. The train conductor came along to sell us tickets, and when addressed in his own language, sat down to have a chat. During the whole of our tour Jim spoke careful grammatical, and sometimes pedantic French when addressing the natives, and I contributed some phrases of 1914–18 *lingua franca* such as 'na poo' and 'san fairy ann'. We took tickets for Bethune and after a few minutes' conversation the conductor rose to leave remarking kindly and sentimentally, 'It is obvious, messieurs, that you make a pilgrimage; though I was not born at the time of the Great War I can understand why you come like many other old Englishmen.'

As we approached Hazebrouck Jim excitedly pointed out a level-crossing where his battalion had suffered its first casualty—a mule—when a limber was hit by a shunting engine as they were detraining in the goods yard, the usual halting place for troop trains, which rarely stopped at proper platforms. There was an elegant newly built railway station at Bethune, but when we emerged from it the town looked unchanged except for some cafés which had been modernized and equipped with blaring juke boxes. The town had suffered some damage in both wars, but the buildings had been restored in the old gabled style.

Bethune, the centre of a mining area, had been the railhead for the Allied positions north of the River Lys, just far enough behind the old front line to be reasonably safe so that tired soldiery could relax there on a few hours' leave from the trenches. As we made our way to the town centre Jim pointed out a house down a side street which had been a brothel—but the red lamp had gone. The market square was still cobbled and its ancient quaint stone tower in the middle stood looking much the same as it has done for centuries. In an *estaminet* we were delighted to find some old advertisements painted on tin plate which might have been hanging there in 1915, and

Jim avowed that that was the place where he had eaten eggs and chips then. As we consumed several bottles of local beer we both commented on the atmosphere and odour of the place. The sense of smell induces memory and nostalgia more than the other senses and we did not need vivid imaginations to hear again the clatter of soldiers' ammunition boots on the *pavé*, the rumbling of horsed transport and the jingling of harness as the evening light slowly failed.

We ate an expensive dinner which included escargots in a good restaurant and Jim ruefully commented that he could have had a whole evening's entertainment in Bethune for five francs in the old days. All the diners except ourselves were locals who had no English so Jim had to summon up all his French when enquiring about hotels. We were directed to the Hotel du Commerce, a very very Gallic establishment, where the cognac was smooth but the beds rough, and we slept little because a wedding party in the dining-room made a fearful din until four o'clock in the morning when the bride and groom departed. As we were sipping our strong coffee and eating croissants at breakfast we decided that we had walked enough on local roads in times past and sent for a taxi. The driver was polite, had no English, but summed us up immediately. '*Messieurs, vous desirez visiter encore les champs du combat — montez messieurs — je vous conduirai à vos amis.*' (Gentlemen, you wish to revisit the battlefields — get in, I shall take you to your friends.) We asked him to drive slowly in the direction of Loos and after two miles he stopped at the gate of a churchyard in the tiny village of Annequin remarking quietly, '*Ici reposent une douzaine soldats Anglais.*' (Here lie a dozen English soldiers.) The church and its burial ground, which was full of the remains of local inhabitants, had survived three great wars including that of 1870. Just inside the iron gates six small headstones facing another six on the other side of the path had been erected by the War Graves Commission. Their simplicity contrasted strangely with other more flamboyant memorials. I thought that they looked like two small military guards formed up for inspection. Jim bent down to read the inscription on the first on the left, then straightened up saying gravely, 'Good heavens here is poor

Corporal Pepperday, one of our first fatal casualties. I was present when he was hit and he died as I was attending to him.' My brother stood for a few moments bareheaded profoundly moved and I feel sure that he said a little prayer, for Jim is truly a practising Christian. When we returned to the taxi he told me the details of the incident as follows, 'We were sheltering from shell-fire in dilapidated buildings in Annequin. I was a stretcher-bearer at the time and went forward with others to pick up a man lying wounded in the open. I remembered my OTC training when we had been told that bursting shrapnel shells could cover an area of a hundred yards by twenty so we dragged him back into a shop before binding him up. A shell burst behind the window and wrecked the place; I was not hit, but a second shell burst in another building just across the road and Pepperday was badly wounded in the neck. When we got to him blood was pulsating from an artery too deep-seated for us to compress. In spite of our efforts we could not arrest the bleeding and after he cried, "Oh my God" and "bloody hell" he quickly subsided and died in my arms. During the following year I was in Annequin again, this time as an officer in the Durham Light Infantry and when I was just about to eat a Christmas Eve dinner of chicken in a farm we were plastered with gas shells but the only casualty was the farmer's horse.'

Jim was very familiar with this part of the front and as we drove along the country roads he pointed out well-known places and buildings now rebuilt with a mixture of new and old bricks. One was a tannery which had been a bath centre where the soldiers had enjoyed themselves soaking in hot water in the vats which were used as communal bath tubs. We stopped and signed our names at several military cemeteries and at one, where many soldiers of the Durham Light Infantry lie buried, Jim walked straight-backed among the graves seeking those of men he had known. I remained in the car chatting to the driver who asked, '*Votre frère, monsieur —quel age a-t-il?*' (How old is your brother, sir?) 'In his eightieth year' I replied, and he continued compassionately, '*Alors, il a bien age — mais regardez il marche comme un jeune soldat au milieu de ses camarades.*' (He is quite old, but look he walks like a young soldier in the midst of his comrades.)

We skirted Hullock and noted some of its towers were still standing. Jim reminisced sadly, 'The Germans held Hullock and I held a small salient with my platoon overlooked by them so it was a dangerous place. It was there that Second Lieutenant Adie of Heaton, Newcastle, who had come from the Argentine as a volunteer, was killed as I was talking to him. A shower of German pineapple mortar grenades fell into the trench bay where we were standing with others and all were killed or wounded except myself and I was left standing covered in yellow TNT.'

As our taxi neared Loos, which our driver pronounced as Loss, we were astonished to hear the sound of bagpipes, and as we entered the village square I recognized the pipers and buglers of the London Irish Rifles wearing their corbeen bonnets, green cloaks, and saffron kilts, countermarching between two lines of elderly bemedalled old comrades of the regiment. These were the survivors of the battle of Loos and this was the fiftieth anniversary of the day when many Territorial regiments suffered their first serious losses on the Western Front. I have some close connections with this regiment and was delighted to meet the present commanding officer, Lieutenant-Colonel Hood, who at first did not recognize me, dressed as I was in sort of ratcatcher clothes. He immediately asked us to join his party and was very interested to learn that Jim had been on the fringes of the battle.

When the music ceased several of us were invited into the Hotel de Ville for a drink with the *Maire*, after which all the party lunched in a large restaurant just outside the town. Colonel Hood remarked at table, 'I have had some difficult jobs in my time but conducting these old chaps, none of them under seventy, has been the most exacting. They started on Guinness in Victoria Station, drank their way across France, and look at them now knocking it back. They are a tougher generation than mine.'

One or two of the veterans were nodding after lunch but the colonel collected them together reminding them that they were to attend a memorial service within an hour. Not one was absent from parade in a huge military cemetery at what they called Dud Corner, where thousands of soldiers of many regiments lie forever in peace. They stood bareheaded between the headstones while their old padre said a few appropriate words and a short prayer, then steadily to attention as the pipers played superbly 'Oft in the stilly night' and some murmured the words. 'Oft in the stilly night, ere slumber's chains have bound me, Fond memories bring the light of other days around me, The eyes that shone, now dimmed and gone, The cheerful hearts now broken.' I have attended many memorial services all over the world, but this simple ceremony in an untidy corner of Flanders, which ended with quavering voices singing the National Anthem touched me more than any.

At sundown the band beat retreat in the village square and performed evolutions which delighted the populace. The parade was reported next day in the *Voix du Nord* with a eulogy which I translated literally as follows: 'The agile presence of the major, the stillness of the drummers, the sharp notes of the bagpipes playing tunes of folklore, the infinite variety of figures on parade impressed all the spectators. With this fanfare — it was all of a civilization, a form of life which was presented to us which interested and moved us.'

After the last bugle note the soldiers and veterans were invited into the Hotel de Ville to drink champagne which the *Maire* and other notables. There were a few speeches and then the local *Curé* asked us to sing 'Tipperary' — curious how this banal song sticks. The French were moved again and responded with 'Madelon', in my opinion a better tune for soldiers. 'Mademoiselle from Armentières' was hushed by the padre, and guests and visitors broke up into groups reminiscing. Like good riflemen the veterans stood fast till all the drink was finished — and our hosts were not niggardly — then dispersed. Outside in the street a young piper was chatting up a willing *jeune fille*; as the pair had no common language the lad asked us to interpret as they exchanged felicitations and addresses. The conversation was cut short by a bellow from the pipe major to fall in. The young piper gallantly whipped off his corbeen bonnet removed the cockade of St Patrick blue feathers, presented it to the lass with a flourish, gave her a smacking kiss and left her. A fragment of verse came into my head, 'There lived a lass, there came a lad, who loved and rode away'.

Though it was now late, Jim and I wished to reach Arras that night so we said our farewells to the old comrades. One, a little drunk, shook hands solemnly and said, 'Ah, we have been wondering who you were — you are two *maquis* and you speak good English for Frenchmen.' We reached Arras in time to eat a late dinner in the Hotel du Strasbourg and book a room after one of the most memorable and interesting days in our lives.

Next morning we delivered a letter from the Mayor of Newcastle-upon-Tyne to his opposite number in Arras, because the two towns are officially linked in friendship, then set out again by car to visit Delville Wood, where South African troops fought and died in one of the bloodiest battles in history. The battleground was now quiet and peaceful, the trees had grown again to their original height in front of a venerable looking farmhouse which looked as though it had stood for centuries, though it had only been rebuilt between the wars in the same fashion as before its destruction in the battle. At our next place of pilgrimage, Vimy Ridge with its astounding war memorial to the Canadian forces, we were surprised to see many picnic parties sitting on the surrounding ground which was still pock-marked with shell craters. Here an extensive area of field works and trenches has been preserved in concrete. It gave us an extraordinary sensation to walk again in the ditches, peep into dug-outs, which smelled as musty as we remembered them, and to lean against the petrified sandbags on the parapets, each one as distinct as when first put into position. Some of these works had been in German hands, and here and there were machine-guns and trench mortars still in their original positions only a few yards away from the British lines.

We decided to make Arras our centre for the rest of the tour as we had pleasant memories of it; a place like Béthune never overrun by the enemy, but providing amenities for soldiers out on rest. The house which was used as an officers' club was still intact and Jim and I recalled we had only missed seeing each other there by a few minutes in 1918. All war damage had been skilfully repaired and the magnificent colonnaded grand square and the Hotel de Ville were well worth seeing again. Except for half a dozen members of the War Graves Commission we were the only Englishmen in the town, as most tourists by-pass it or speed through on their way to the sun. Immediately outside the actual town the countryside was curiously empty when we drove south-west into it, over a well-remembered level-crossing, but on every signpost we read familiar names of little hamlets which had been just piles of powdered rubble in 1917. The distances between them which we thought unending when we marched now seemed absurdly short.

At Flesquieres, now rebuilt and quite charming, Jim had gone forward with the 2nd Bn the Durham Light Infantry following up the tank attack which was so successful on the first day of the Cambrai battle. He recognized the exact spot where he had crossed a tiny stream on the start line, by the remains of two piers supporting a culvert. 'To see this spot,' said he putting his hands in the water, 'is worth the whole expense of this trip.' There was no one about in the village except in a small *estaminet* where we drank some beer. None of the customers remembered the old village but were interested in our explorations and were most kind to us, listening to our tales.

I told our driver to take the road to Bullecourt, Ecoust and Croisilles and discovered there were many cemeteries on the way. In one, isolated from others, were graves of Chinese who had served in labour battalions and died so far from their homeland. The headstones seemed even more pathetic than others and perhaps never visited.

Our taxi, the only car on the road, ascended a little rising ground which quickly fell away and I suddenly shouted 'stop' as I saw that we were skirting a cutting with a light railway running along it. The driver pulled up at a small signal box which had been a pile of bricks when I last saw it on 21st March, 1918. This was the place where the Germans had taken me prisoner. Using the box as a guide I located the exact spots where dreadful things had happened on that day. The trenches had long disappeared under years of cultivation but I knew for certain the sites of Battalion HQ and A Company dug-out in front of which the stretcher party had been decimated. We sat on the side of the cutting above it while I described the battle as I saw it. The rising ground over which we had come was the area where we had first seen the enemy behind us and the shallow trench in which we had crouched during the preliminary bombardment had been sited within a few yards of where we were sitting. All was silent and peaceful now, the land was in stubble with wild flowers growing in profusion, and there was no house or person in sight. It was a lovely sunny day so we sat for twenty minutes till the silence was broken by the report of a shotgun from the direction of the old German front line—it was only a *chasseur* shooting at a hare. 'Come,' said Jim, 'it is time to go.' He picked some wild flowers and a sprig of rosemary from a small bush growing at his side then rose to his feet saying, 'We'll take these for remembrance.'

On our way back to Arras we stopped at a miniature burial ground containing only a few graves, which looked unusual. I read the inscription on one headstone, 'Second Lieutenant —— The Royal Northumberland Fusiliers (Tyneside Scottish Battalion) aged 19 killed 1944.' This boy, the same age as I was in 1918, had fallen in another war serving in my own regiment, and I had lived to read his epitaph. This affected me so much that I said to Jim, 'We shall visit no more graveyards but look for places of which we have pleasant memories.'

Next day, in a one-coach diesel train, we meandered through the country, halting at tiny stations with names familiar as villages where troops on rest from the lines had been billeted. One, Tinques, brought back an amusing memory. There had been an RFC airfield near by to which on one occasion the battalion's officers had been invited to dinner. Rather than let us walk there, the squadron's cheery mess president had said, 'No—you poor bloody infantry can ride for a change,' and sent Crossley tenders to transport us. We arrived in the middle of a mild German air raid, but were

immediately ushered to the mess and plied with glasses of
gin which were refilled before they were empty. A superb
dinner, by our infantry standards, was served with a full
bottle of wine for each guest with the injunction that it be
finished before the port was passed and the loyal toast proposed. A rugby match followed, with a hassock as the ball,
much to the detriment of the furniture, after which more to
drink and songs from *The Bing Boys*, *Chu Chin Chow* and
some RFC bawdy ones accompanied by the mess president at
the piano. At some time past midnight the squadron commander called a halt as some of his pilots were detailed for a
dawn patrol. Several battalion officers were casualties due to
alcohol or the game but the mess president thoughtfully provided stretchers and an ambulance for our return trip to our
billets. I look back on this evening as the cheeriest I spent on
the Western Front but because of the lavish RFC hospitality,
not the least risky.

Jim and I left the train at St Pol which we remembered as a
pleasant little town where our elder brother Alec had been
stationed at a hospital for some months, and I had ridden fifteen miles on our company charger to visit him. The place
had been almost entirely rebuilt after destruction in the
Second World War and we found no landmarks except one
rather tatty *estaminet* near the station. It was called the Victoria and looked as though it had been built during the last
century. Jim made a gaffe by asking the *propriétrice* if she remembered the First World War, and got a sharpish reply,
'*Mon Dieu*, I am not as old as that.' We fell in with a couple of
old boozers who did remember, and we spent a long session
reminiscing and drinking beer. They tried to restrain us when
we said we really must catch a train back to Arras, swearing
that there was a later one, but Jim made a good exit line
quoting an old French saying, '*Si vous voulez de l'amour, ne
restez pas huit jours — mais prenez le train qui file.*' (If you wish
to make love, do not wait eight days, but catch the train as it
speeds.)

Breakfasting in our hotel on our last morning there we
came to the conclusion that it was a miracle that we three
brothers who had spent a total of seven years on the Western

Front all survived without much hurt, while some families we knew had lost all their sons.

We settled our bill and said adieu to the kindly *madame propriétrice*; Jim preceded me out into the street stepping briskly as usual. I slung my pack on to my shoulders, and as I followed him I heard madame whisper to the waitress, '*Regardez, Jeannette — les deux vieux frères — les combatants anciens marchent encore.*' (Look, Jeannette — the two old brothers — the old combatants march again.)

Chapter 17

FAREWELL TO ARMS

Alnwick Castle stands in Northumberland, midway between Tyne and Tweed, and was for centuries a bastion against Scottish invaders, and a place where the English assembled for raids across the border into Scotland. The keep was there when Flodden was fought, and before that time, when the Percy's and Harry Hotspur were powers in the land. Throughout its long history, it has been closely associated with warfare and with men-at-arms, and during the two world wars many soldiers encamped in its grounds. It is the seat of the Duke of Northumberland, who donated one of the towers on the outer walls for a regimental museum.

On 2nd May, 1970, another concourse of soldiers paraded there — two companies of The Royal Northumberland Fusiliers (The Fighting Fifth), who came to lay up in perpetuity the colours of its 1st Battalion, which had recently been merged with other famous regiments, after nearly three hundred years' service as a separate corps. No place could be more fitting or traditional as a home for these precious relics, which are now on view to the public.

Hundreds of ex-members of the regiment and numerous other spectators assembled to witness the ceremony, which took place on the brilliant green sward of the outer bailey, overlooked by the stone sculptures of armed men which had been placed centuries ago on the battlements to simulate sentries on the look-out for Scottish raiders. The grey outer walls, on three sides, formed a magnificent background to the parade, which was very colourful as the drummers were in full scarlet dress with fusilier seal-skin caps, with the troops in modern uniforms with red and white hackles in their blue berets.

My brothers, Alex and Jim, stood shoulder-to-shoulder with me in the front rank of the veterans, our ages totalling almost two hundred and forty years. A unique, as well as memorable, occasion, it was the first time that we had all stood on parade together; and it was sixty-four years since Alex, the eldest, had first worn a scarlet tunic in a volunteer battalion of the regiment.

As the colour party marched on to the parade ground, I recalled a similar occasion forty-eight years before, when I had carried the King's Colour of the 22nd Battalion to be laid up in St Nicholas Cathedral, Newcastle-upon-Tyne, where it still hangs. We three brothers looked with discerning eyes at the stalwart young fusiliers formed up in review order, and we decided that they looked staunch professionals, very different from the amateur and temporary soldiers with which we had served. Their drill was more precise too, and it was obvious that every officer and man on parade was doing his utmost to make the ceremony faultless, and to be a credit to their regiment.

During the short divine service which was conducted by the chaplains, I feel sure that most of those present were thinking of the many who had followed the banners throughout three centuries, and of the many thousands of them who lie in graves in distant lands. Later, my brother Alex remarked, 'That ceremonial and pageantry is part of the history of England — a small fragment, and a sad one.'

At the conclusion of the service, the uniformed men presented arms, and the veterans stood bareheaded, as the Queen's Colour of red, white and blue, and the regimental one of gosling green, were trooped along the lines for the last time. Then, to the tune of 'Auld Lang Syne', were slow-marched to the Abbot's Tower and faded away through the arch in its grey stone walls.

The veterans were inspected, almost individually, by the Duke and by Field-Marshal Festing; and then the whole parade formed up in column of route and marched past a saluting base, as the band played the regimental march, 'The British Grenadiers', we then dispersed to refreshments. As they were consumed, everyone reminiscing, the musicians played folk tunes of the county, concluding with the famous 'Blaydon Races'.

It was the end of another epoch, so this is perhaps a fitting moment for the sentimental author of these memoirs to end this book and to fade away himself.

Appendix

THE ROAD TO OONOESWHERE
by
Sir Alan Herbert 1918

There's a village in the distance, we'll be gettin' there tonight
And perhaps we'll have an easy, and perhaps we'll have a fight
We don't know what we're doin, and we ain't supposed to
care
We always knows we're always on the road to Oonoeswhere.
On the road to Oonoeswhere, there may be billets there
Or if there isn't, there'll be lots of open air
Lots of jolly open air, we can bivvy in the square,
But our cooker's ditched behind us, and it's very hard to
bear.

We walks along and wonders what it's all about
We hopes that someone savvys, but at times we have our
doubt.
When the adjutant looks worried and the colonel seems in
pain
We whispers in our sorrow 'Gawd he's lost himself again'
On the road to Oonoeswhere, course it isn't our affair
But I wish some gent would tell 'em, how to get to
Oonoeswhere.

We 'alts at level-crossings and has a lovely view
Of 'igh class trains a shuntin', but they ain't for me and you
We only rides on railways when there's dirty work ahead,
And if we rides on motors it means we're nearly dead.
It means you're nearly dead, with your belly full of lead
And a ticket on your tunic 'this man must not be fed'.

But the colonel sits his mare and it don't seem hardly fair
That we cannot all get horses on the road to Oonoeswhere.

And when our backs are breakin' and death seems very near,
We marches to attention, and inspects the brigadier,
He sees our tin hats polished and our hypes got up to please
But if he saw our blisters, we'd all be OBEs
Bloomin' blistered OBEs, all a wobbling at the knees,
First we sweat like rivers and then we stands to freeze.
   On the road to Oonoeswhere, ah que voulez c'est la guerre
Only this 'ere step they're settin' is enough to make you
                          swear.

But the old sun comes out sometime and the poplars climb
                       the hill
Like a lot of silly soldiers at extended order drill.
And there's bits of wood and scenery, and the war don't seem
                       so near
And the band plays through a village, and the kids come out
                       to cheer
Aye the kids come out to cheer, and a man feels kind of
                       queer,
And the girls they blow you kisses, and mothers brings you
                       beer.
   On the road to Oonoeswhere, aye it warnt all skittles there
But sometimes I wish I was back again on the road to
                       Oonoeswhere.